I S

with my little eye

BY

BARRY R. SMITH

Note well: "Whether they are aware of it or unaware of it, any individual or group working towards a One World Government is either part of, or an agent of, Weishaupt's Illuminati conspiracy." P. Aristarchus.

Published by Barry Smith Family Evangelism
Pelorus Bridge, Rai Valley
Marlborough, New Zealand
Ph. 64-3-571 6046 Fax 64-3-571 6135
ISBN 0-908961-07-3

Contents

Dedication

I finished writing this manuscript during the month of November, 1999 and gladly dedicate it to the lady who carried me for nine months; looked after me so well until I was old enough to leave home, and along with my dad, Ted Smith, prayed that I would live through a life-threatening operation at the age of only 8 days old.

You gave me to the Lord and I lived.

You've been on this earth for 93 years now, Mum, and Heaven is just through the door. I love you, Vera Annie Smith.

Barry.

Preface

Some years ago, I was engaged in teaching music at a well-known Auckland, New Zealand, high school. Entering my room one morning, full of vim and vigour, I was brought up short by a dreadful odour assailing my nostrils. Would you believe it? A rat had passed away behind a stack of instruments in the store-room!

Tongue in cheek, I approached my head of department for advice as to what to do next. "I believe a rat has died in my store-room," I said, "and I am sticking to the rules by approaching you for your advice, and I might mention, assistance, during this time of crisis."

With a twinkle in his eye, my superior replied, "Mr Smith, this is one occasion in which I feel quite justified in delegating authority," and then he walked away chuckling to himself.

All over the world today, people can smell the proverbial rat, but they are struggling to find the source of the stench. This rat is a **highly organised and motivated group**, controlled by a secret society called the **Illuminati**. The players are many, and were called by George Bush in his pre-Gulf War speech in 1990, "**a thousand points of light**."

For the past 15 years until 1999, they have used the un-proven philosophies of think tanks, some of them based in Europe i.e. the Adam Smith Institute and the Mont Pelerin Society, along with the Centre for Independent Studies in Australia.

They used a small country in the South Pacific called New Zealand, as their **laboratory**. The terrible cost of this experiment has been despair and even suicide, yet in the opinion of the instigators, it has proven itself to be a great success.

Late in 1999, the stealing of New Zealand's national sovereignty is almost complete, and so, they have now exported the same plan to many other countries. They spread the lie to people in these other nations that the New Zealand experiment was an un-qualified success. For New Zealand citizens, it was not, but for the Illuminati conspirators and their wealthy friends, it was!

"The triumphing of the wicked is short."[1] Many of these persons have made a great deal of money out of their destructive business, however, they have only a brief period of time to enjoy their ill-gotten gains.

George Bush called the plan, **New World Order**, but Jimmy Carter before him put a time constraint on it. His name for it was **Global 2000**.

I encourage you to keep reading. The Titanic looked good too until she went down!

Statement

By the 1st January 2000, the economy as we know it today, will cease to exist!

---

[1]Job 20:5

Foreword
Danger - Danger
Date - March 1985 - San Jose, California, U.S.A

The shrill ringing of the phone at 11:30 p.m. told me that something serious was happening or about to happen. As soon as I picked up the receiver, I knew that my suspicions were well-founded. The voice of an acquaintance spoke quietly yet urgently. *"You have really stirred up a hornet's nest over here. The Freemasons are extremely angry and have threatened vengeance. There have been plans made to get you at San Francisco airport. I'm warning you. Please take this very seriously!"*

We had just concluded some 39 lectures in venues all over the United States. A very angry man had confronted me at the conclusion of one of these meetings. I began to realise that the situation was becoming very volatile, and thus found sleep virtually impossible for the rest of the night.

Not wishing to alarm anybody else in the house, I kept the information I had received strictly to myself, yet at the same time, I was not quite sure what my next move should be. Suddenly, some words which I had heard many years before came to mind. *"But when they persecute you in this city, flee ye into another."*[1] In other words, if trouble is brewing, and you can feel it in the air, do not stay on to fight; go for your life!

Realising that this course of action meant sacrificing my return fares home to the tune of approximately $3000, I didn't cancel the bookings that I had already made but re-booked on another airline, out through Canada, and on home to New Zealand via Great Britain.

I must confess to a tremendous feeling of relief as the plane's wheels left the tarmac at Vancouver airport. True, I had lost the money, yet secured my life for a further season.

Critics at this point may accuse me of lack of faith in God

or humanity, or even cowardice. However, the words of an Australian lecturer return to assist me from time to time. *"He who fires his pop-gun and runs away, lives to fire his pop-gun another day."*

Since the U.S. experience, there have been many more stories to tell of unusual happenings in our dealings with not only Freemasons but also other occultists and satanic individuals. I include one more such story herewith. This incident was not only printed in the 'Fiji Times', on the 22nd June 1993, but also in the New Zealand Herald on the 25th June, 1993 - *"Satanic link upsets diplomat.*

A senior American diplomat walked out of a presidential prayer meeting in Suva on Saturday after a guest speaker compared some American leaders with satanic practices.

President Ratu Sir Penaia Ganilau did not attend. Charge d'affaires Michael Marine walked out after guest speaker Barry Smith, a New Zealand evangelist, made the comparison. Government House is seeking clarification from the organisers.

The President's aide-de-camp, Major Sakiusa Raivoce, said the President's office wanted to know who organised the breakfast and what happened.

"Someone is bound to ask the President what happened and intend to hear from the organisers.

"Barry Smith, who is not a local, made some statements that hurt some people - if we allow things like this to happen, people will not want to come anymore."

Mr Smith was invited to speak at the prayer breakfast at the Suva Travelodge on Saturday.

The director of the United States Information Service at the American Embassy in Suva, Charla Hatton said invitations to the breakfast were made in the name of the President.

"Mr Marine said Mr Smith had made allegations that our past governments and some of our founders had some satanic policies," she said.

"He even linked some past United States leaders to satanic practices."

"His thesis," according to Mr Marine, "is that there is a worldwide conspiracy to form a single government under Satan, and the U.S. is one country pushing for it."

Mrs Hatton said Mr Marine found the statements slanderous and was deeply offended.

"However, he has identified one of the organisers and has written to him, expressing disappointment about the statements," she said.

"Until the incident, Mr Marine had found the breakfast spiritually enriching."

Mrs Hatton could not confirm reports that other guests had also left after Mr Smith continued his barrage against the US government.

He was sorry that such an illustrious group of Fiji citizens had to be subjected to such eccentric views.

"His statements were offensive but they were made by an individual. He offended not only Mr Marine but the whole country."

Mrs Hatton said the U.S. was a country that accommodated any religion, and encouraged freedom of speech.

"However, Mr Smith was extremely offensive to the country," she said.

The prayer breakfast was filled to capacity; attendance was estimated at about 80 guests." End quote.

All this strikes me as very strange behaviour and certainly not logical. For instance, when the doctor tells you that you have cancer, stalking out of his surgery with a hurt look on your face in no ways alters the fact that you still have the cancer. A better approach, I suggest, would be to seek a second opinion, and if it is deemed necessary, a cure.

Let us say that my vocation is extremely exciting if nothing else!

---

[1]Matthew 10:23

Chapter One
Cairo, Egypt - Witchcraft

(The information from the following scenario has been taken from articles from the 'Sunday Times', Western Australia, 8th November 1998 and 'Daily Mail', London, 23rd July 1999.)

It is 11:50 p.m. on the 31st December 1999. The stillness of the desert night is shattered with the throbbing of helicopter blades. Only able to be identified by a spotlight cutting a swathe through the blackness of the night, it now descends and hovers over the Great Cheops Pyramid at Giza.

A gasp escapes from many lips as it suddenly becomes apparent as to its purpose. A giant canvas sling is being lowered and then, the crowd catches their first sight of the cargo contained therein. Spotlights are suddenly turned on, and there, gleaming in the beams of these lights, supported temporarily in the canvas sling is a 9 metre golden coloured capstone.

The excitement is infectious and the crowds surge forward to view this strange phenomena. The word soon gets around that this golden capstone will restore this structure, one of the seven wonders of the world, to its original 137 metres, if only for a period of 8 hours, when at sunrise on January 1st 2000, the same helicopter will whisk it away again to an unknown destination.

A fairy tale? Unfortunately not. This is a highly-planned event, with a very sinister purpose behind it.

Then at midnight, just as the capstone rests in position, Egyptologist Robert Bauval, will appear on a platform in front of the Sphinx, accompanied by a group known as "the Magic 21" and will announce the return of the ancient gods to Egypt.

At the same time all this is taking place, a group of world planners with their secret agenda ready to be fulfilled will make their way up the board-walk, inside the pyramid, known as the ascending passage. They will congregate in a room known as the King's Chamber, and horror of horrors, conduct an unholy invocation **proclaiming the year 2000 as the year of the Antichrist.**

The first year of the New Age of the Antichrist will be represented by the numerical symbol 0 with the abbreviations AA for Anno Antichristus (Year of the Antichrist).

Aleister Crowley 666

In the month of March 1904, when the notorious black magician, Aleister Crowley, went to Cairo on his honeymoon, he spent a whole night performing magical rites in the King's Chamber of the Great Pyramid. And when he and his wife Rose, went to the Cairo Museum, she led him straight to a wooden structure of the god **Horus**, labelled with a number he regarded as his personal logo - 666 - the Beast in Revelations. (Please remember that the eye in the triangle on the reverse side of the US$1 is representative of the eye of Horus.)

Soon after that, a mysterious voice spoke from the air and dictated Crowley's most famous work *"The Book of the Law"* with its invocation. ***"Do what thou wilt shall be the whole law."*** End quote.

Do you realise the purport of what you have just read? This author is racing to finish this book and get it out to the public before the 31st December 1999. Why? Because within a period of two months (Nov/Dec 1999), nobody will be buying books as the Old Word Order comes to a close and the New World Order commences on the 1st January 2000.

Chapter Two
The Significance of the Great Pyramid at Giza

In our book, 'The Devil's Jigsaw', on page 170-178, we pointed out the fact that this great structure, situated on the border of North and South Egypt, is sometimes labelled, **the "history of the world in stone"**. We point out that the prophet Isaiah refers to this structure in four ways (see Isaiah 19:19-20).

➤   An altar
➤   A pillar
➤   A sign
➤   A witness to the Lord of Hosts in the midst of the land of Egypt

The capstone, however, is missing , as it represents the Son of the living God, our Lord Jesus Christ. This, our great Saviour, Lord and Master, has been once to this earth in the form of **a suffering Servant**. The Jewish prophets agree that He will return later in history as **the reigning King**. As temporary blindness is on most of modern day Israel, they cannot spiritually perceive these two separate comings.

"Blindness in part is happened to Israel, until the fulness of the Gentiles be come in."[1]

"But He was wounded for our transgressions, He was bruised for our iniquities: the chastisement of our peace was upon Him; and with His stripes we are healed."[2]   Stage 1.

"And the Lord shall be king over all the earth: in that day shall there be one Lord, and His Name one."[3]   Stage 2.

You see, we need a Saviour first because we are all sinners and the wages of sin is death. Never forget however, that the gift of God is eternal life. Later on, those who have accepted Him willingly and have asked Him to be their Lord and Saviour, will be in a very good position. Unfortunately, the same cannot be said for those who neglect or outright reject His great salvation.

3

Our Lord Jesus Christ is both the chief corner stone and the capstone of history. He is the first and the last, the beginning and the end, the alpha and omega, He began everything and He will finish everything.

Now for an explanation of the lowering of the golden capstone on to the Great Cheops Pyramid at Giza on the 31st December 1999. At the same time, our secret world planners gather in the very same place where Aleister Crowley spent a whole night (March 1904). This group of frighteningly deceived individuals, all created in the image of Almighty God, and made for His pleasure, will commit **the ultimate blasphemy**. Led by top Freemasons, whose calendar goes under the heading, "A.L.", or "In the Year of Lucis/Lucifer", the luciferian invocation will be pronounced. During a lecture tour of Ireland in October, 1999, this was handed to me. http://www.tgd.org/oai/anticrst.html

The Luciferian Invocation

"The Manifesto of the Order of the Antichristian Illuminati - O.A.I. - Ordo Antichristianus Illuminati", by David Cherubim (G.H. Frater O.A.I.) The Antichrist 666, 1996 e.v.

"Come unto me, o ye children of the Sun, and I, the Antichrist, shall uplift ye to the Palace of the Stars, where all is Light, and Life, and Love, and Liberty!"

Do what thou wilt shall be the whole of the Law."
(Author's note - Isn't this Aleister Crowley's statement?)

*"First, let the Aspirant to our Holy Order read herein the **Manifesto of the O.A.I.**, to gain knowledge and insight regarding the structure, system and philosophy of the Order. Next, let the Aspirant read the **Manifesto of the Antichrist**, and also **Liber Antichristus**, The Book of the Antichrist, which is the principle Holy Book of the **Order of the Antichristian Illuminati**. Then, let the Aspirant read **Diary of the Antichrist** (Number 1), which is the Sacred Record of the Life and Spirit of the ANTICHRIST, whose time is now at hand; and let the Aspirant extract from this Sacred Record the Knowledge and Wisdom which imparts the Understanding of the Universal Mysteries of the Spirit of the ANTICHRIST.*

Also, let the Aspirant know the history of our Holy Order, *which was founded through the True Will of a Thelemic Magician, who has been an High Initiate of various Magical and Occult Orders, and who is the Chief Officer and Representative of the Aleister Crowley Foundation (A.C.F.) in both the USA and Canada, and the Founder, Chief and International Grand Master of the Thelemic Order of the Golden Dawn (**Order of T.G.D.**), which is an international Magical and Occult Organization founded on the Vernal Equinox of 1990 e.v., and which is dedicated to the establishment of the Law of Thelema, which is the Law of the **Beast 666**. The **O.A.I.** derives its Official Link and Spiritual Authority from the Magical Sanctuary of the Order of the **T.G.D.** (**Thelemic Golden Dawn**), called the Inner Order of the **R.C.** (**Rose Cross**), which itself is but the representation on a lower plane of the Eternal Order of the **A.A.**"* (Author's note - The Rose Cross or Rose Croix is the 18th degree in Freemasonry.)

*"The **O.A.I.** is a symbol of the **New World Order** which is now emerging in the world of men and women, preparing for the New Age of the ANTICHRIST, which will, in the minds of the profane, **arise on the first day of the year A.D. 2000. A new calendar will commence** on this day, to accord with this doctrine of the New Age. The first year of the New Age of the ANTICHRIST will be represented by the numberical symbol 0 with the abbreviations A.A. for **Anno Antichristus** (Year of the Antichrist). And the ANTICHRIST will reign upon the earth, causing all men and women to worship the **Law of Liberty**. Christianity will become obsolete, and an evil upon the earth; and the Christians will forsake their false god and worship the ANTICHRIST as Lord of the World."* (Author's note - A sad misapprehension.)

*"The ANTICHRIST is an Universal Principle whose work is to free humanity from the fatal restrictions of Christianity and to make possible for all men and women the essential opportunity to know and to be the gods that they are, to live freely and joyously according to their own true natures in the New Age of the ANTICHRIST. The real law of the obsolete Christian religion was restriction. But only in freedom can we perform and accomplish the Great Work of Human and Spiritual Evolution. The Law of the ANTICHRIST is the **Law of Liberty** which makes for the dynamic growth of all. It is the **Law of Thelema** — that is, the Law of Will*

— which emancipates men and women from the evil fetters of restriction, aligning their soul, mind and body with the essential and creative ways of Nature and the Universe.

*The **O.A.I.** is dedicated to the propagation and preservation of the Works of the ANTICHRIST, who was the **Anointed Cherub** of God, **Lucifer**, the Light-Bearer and Morning Star, the Seal of Perfection, full of wisdom and perfect in Beauty, but who, with fierce angelic pride, rebelled against the Most High and fell from grace, and with him a third of the Angels of Heaven, and who is now the **Prince of the Power of the Air**, the **Seed of Satan**, the **Son of BAPHOMET**, the **Child of the Beast 666**, the **Proclaimer of the New World Order**, and the **Dark Lord of the Great Tribulation** who shall cause the people of the earth to worship the **Beast 666**, to forsake the false religion of Christianity, and to spiritually initiate the New Millennial Kingdom of the ANTICHRIST from the draconian depths of the Human Psyche. The ANTICHRIST was born in a physical body on October 24, 1964 e.v., 44 minutes in the Sign of Scorpio, in the City of LA (Los Angeles), in the State of California of the United States of America."* (Author's note - As we are dealing with Satan here, this statement is not necessarily correct, but may have been inserted to mislead Christians.) *"Scorpio is Typhon-Apophis-Set, and 44 is the special number of the Egyptian God Horus, the Crowned and Conquering Child of Force and Fire. The ANTICHRIST is both **Set** and **Horus**, Two-in-One, the Lord of Double Power. The **O.A.I.** is the **Antichristian Current of Set-Heru** (Set and Horus)."* (Author's note - Dualism - two in one. Note the checkered Freemasons' Lodge floor.)

*"All members of the **O.A.I.** accept the Founder of the Order as the Physical Incarnation of the ANTICHRIST, and as the Chief Authority and Grand Master of the Order, entrusted by the Secret Chiefs of the **A.A.** to both rule and constitute the Order. The Grand Master of the Order is publicly known in the world of men and women by the name **David Cherubim**, but whose magical name in the Order is **G.H. Frater O.A.I.** to signify his position as the Founder of the Order. The Sacred Emblem of His High Office as the Grand Master of the **O.A.I.** is the **Eagle of Liberty**, which is also our Sacred Emblem for the **New World Order**, which is the*

Antichristian Order of the Liberated Ones.

*All members of the **O.A.I.** are Self-Willed Antichristians, that is, they are voluntarily dedicated to the spiritual emancipation of themselves and all of humanity from the Evil of the World — Christianity! — through the proper application of the **Law of Liberty** and the creative execution of the dynamic principle of Revolution. The **Law of Liberty** is the Law of Thelema, that is, "**DO WHAT THOU WILT**", which asserts that a WoMan should know and be the god that s/he is, living according to the unique formula of his/her own True Will.*

*All members of the **O.A.I.** are Self-Will Citizens of the **New World Order**, which is, in Antichristendom, the Unification of all Nations, Races, Tribes, Peoples, and Religions in One Universal Spirit — the Eternal Spirit of Freedom! The **New World Order** is ultimately dedicated to the dynamic creation of an Universal Nation, a New Race and a New Religion which embraces all Nations, Races, Tribes, Peoples, and Religions in the Eternal Spirit of Freedom. **But to accomplish this Great Work of Human and Spiritual Evolution we must annihilate the Evil of the World — Christianity!**"* (Author's note - What a hopeless task!) " *— **which falsely proclaims itself to be the One True Religion**, negating, and thus separating itself from, all other Religions and Peoples. Christianity has been the one great curse and corruption of the human spirit, and the principal cause of human division, restriction and suffering in the world. Ergo, it is the complete antithesis of the Spirit of the ANTICHRIST, which is universal in kind, embracing and liberating all things under the Great Sun of Eternal Joy!*

*The **New World Order** is the manifestation of a New World Philosophy of Independence and Freedom. As Citizens of the **New World Order** , we are to be self-governed, autonomous beings, liberated from all political, racial and religious impositions and restrictions, free to govern and to control our own lives in accordance with our own inner natures. This Philosophy is ecumenical or global in nature, and all-embracing in kind; and it is the annihilation of all those false religious and political systems of thinking and living which bar us from the Truth of the Unity of all things. It is the Understanding of the necessity for diversity in the world, and it is Wisdom that such diversity constitutes the Spirit of*

*Unity. It is the realization that all men and women are unequal, and that such inequality constitutes the actual freedom of the individual and the only true form of liberty among men and women. The Law of the **New World Order** is the **Law of Liberty**, which is the Law of the **Beast 666**, which permits for the free expression of each individual in the world, allowing for each individual to discover and pursue their own True Will or Path in Life. This Law demands that we free ourselves of all standard ways and codes of conduct, that we exist by way of our own inner light, and that we calculate our own unique orbits in the Universe.*

...Every man and every woman is a Star, that is, a self-sufficient Centre of light and power,....

...It is entirely a process of Self-Initiation. The way of the ANTICHRIST is the way of the Self....

*...The Magical Symbol of the O.A.I. is the **Mark of the Beast 666**, which is the Union of the Cross and Circle, and it represents the Great Work of the Magick of the **Beast 666**. It is also the **Mark of Initiation**, and the **Mark of Ra-Hoor-Khuit**, who is the Lord of Initiation. Every member of the O.A.I. must have this Great and Holy Symbol tattooed upon his/her body as a token of his/her initiation into the Antichristian Current of the O.A.I....*

*It is the Word of **HOOR** (Horus)....*

....10. And lo! I come up out of the earth, having two horns like a lamb, and I speak as a dragon! It is I, the ANTICHRIST....making every man and every woman a god in their own right.....There is no God but Man.

*...Thus are all men and woman made one with my Father **BAPHOMET**, in me, on earth; and in this unity of force there is lust & joy on earth in the rapture of freedom...."* End quote.

How do you like that? A demonic outburst of uncontrollable anger and audacity. Any child of the true and living God will recognise the arrogant spirit behind this statement. Many times, over the years, as we have cast out evil spirits from men and women in the Name of, and through the power of, the Lord Jesus Christ, these demons use the person's voice to propagate their unmitigated drivel. None of their words warrant the slightest attention as our Lord Jesus Christ has already won the victory over

Satan and all his demon forces as He hung on the cross and shed His precious blood.

"...*the devil is come down unto you having great wrath because he knoweth he hath but a short time.*"[4]

"*And having spoiled principalities and power, He* (Christ) *made a shew of them openly, triumphing over them in it.*"[5]

With this in mind, make perfectly sure in your own heart who you are following -

a)   Jesus = Heaven forever
b)   Lucifer/Satan = Hell forever

---

[1]Romans 11:25
[2]Isaiah 53:5
[3]Zechariah 14:9
[4]Revelation 12:12b
[5]Colossians 2:15

Chapter Three
Time, Gentlemen Please

Some years ago in our country New Zealand, the laws on licensed premises all took effect at 6.00 p.m. each evening. The proprietor would call out in the politest of tones, **"Time, gentlemen please."**

As I pen this, my seventh book, in late 1999, so many of the predictions we have made previously have come to pass and I feel that it is appropriate to give a recap or a broad overview of what we have said in these books since the year 1978. For further light on each statement, we will endeavour to give some resource material.

In the year 1972, on the island of Rarotonga in the Cook Islands, I had a supernatural encounter with God, and I received instructions as to how to get this message out.

Divine Instructions

Not being a super-spiritual individual nor even one given to bringing the Name of God into every conversation, it is important that I include this story at this point so that the reader may understand, it was never my desire to seek out all this information, let alone share it with audiences world-wide!

This particular afternoon, I was kneeling alongside my bed in a little cottage situated amongst the banana and coconut trees up the Takuvaine Valley behind the capital Avarua, Rarotonga in the Cook Islands.

For some time, I felt an increasing urgency to bring the little information that had come to my attention to the notice of my own people of New Zealand and Australia since it affected them. However, how does one get on the lecture circuit with a message such as this one? Possibly an ad in the paper stating, "My name is Smith. Here I am you lucky people!"

There are a number of disadvantages with this approach, number one being that there is a Smith behind every bush. Secondly, because the words "God" and "Jesus" appear regularly in all these publications, many readers suspect that the information presented does not warrant their serious consideration. In these cases, the books, to their minds, contain the ravings of a mentally unstable religious nutter. The strange thing is that these same individuals, when lying on their death-beds, call for help to make their peace with God. Thirdly, secular bookshops in the main refuse to stock these books which leaves your average citizen in the sad position of never finding out the true facts of **this giant world-wide conspiracy**. Sadly, these seekers after knowledge are left with another option, i.e. talk-back radio, where people spend hour after hour feeding each other's ignorance.

However, back to my story.

Whilst in this kneeling position and crying out to God for direction, I began to shake as the power of the Lord flowed through me. I flicked open my Living Bible to **Habakkuk 2:2-3** and my tears splashed on the open page as I read these words. *"...Write my answer on a billboard, large and clear, so that anyone can read it at a glance and rush to tell the others. But these things I plan won't happen right away. Slowly, steadily, surely, the time approaches when the vision will be fulfilled. If it seems slow, do not despair, for these things will surely come to pass. Just be patient! They will not be overdue a single day!"* End quote.

I continued to cry and tremble for some time after that, then stumbled in to the shower, hoping that the cold water would give me back my strength.

A few days later, upon our arrival back in New Zealand, in obedience to the divine instructions, I printed a little prophetic pamphlet, then later a series of six books, this one making it seven.

Reactions to the Books

Stories abound from positive to negative responses. Men, in particular, are influenced by the irrefutable information and tens of thousands have been forced to rethink their world-view. An interesting comment seems applicable at this point.

If you haven't changed your opinion about anything over the last five years, feel your pulse - you may be dead!

Prime Ministers and Presidents have read these books and attended our lectures - in most cases declaring that this material is correct. They should know, shouldn't they?

Do yourself a favour and please read this book slowly and carefully. The results could be life-changing.

Do Not Pre-judge

People are continually approaching me with this phrase on their lips, "Would you please forgive me for pre-judging you and the message that you have carried over the years."
The interesting point here is that 99% of my critics have never attended my lectures, nor read the books. The wisest man who ever lived put it this way. *"He that answereth a matter before he heareth it, it is folly and shame unto him."*[1]

In 722 B.C. the prophet had my concerns also - *"My people are destroyed through lack of knowledge."*[2]

---

[1]Proverbs 18:13
[2]Hosea 4:6

Chapter Four
Recap and Precis

It was predicted in about the year A.D.51 that terrible changes in the social, economic and structural order of the earth would change, preparing the way for the rise of a final world dictator. His title, - Antichrist. The numeric value of his name - 666.

"And now ye know what withholdeth that he might be revealed in his time. For the mystery of iniquity doth already work and he who now letteth will let until he be taken out of the way."[1] End quote.

"Here is wisdom, let him that hath understanding count the number of the beast, for it is the number of a man, and his number is six hundred, three score and six."[2] - 666. End quote.

We've arrived, folks. The mystery of iniquity is ready to be fulfilled. The world is under siege by Luciferian forces. *"The devil is come down unto you, having great wrath, because he knoweth he hath but a short time."*[3] End quote.

Q.   How does he know that he has a short time?
A.   He can read the prophecies.

Facts

Fact 1 - On the reverse side of every U.S. dollar printed since 1933, we have the seals of the Illuminati, a secret society set up in Bavaria on May 1st 1776, by an ex-Jesuit Adam Weishaupt. (See Encyclopaedia Britannica, Vol 12, 1963.)

Fact 2 - The Illuminati founders' aim was to get rid of religion and replace it with reason. (See Encyclopaedia Britannica, Vol 12, 1963.)

Fact 3 - Through his friend Baron Von Knigge, Weishaupt infiltrated the Freemasons' Lodges with his luciferian ideas. (See Encyclopaedia Britannica, Vol 12, 1963.) Men in the upper degrees only were instructed.

Fact 4 - Both seals on the reverse side of the U.S.$1 bill are a mass of occult and Masonic symbolism. (See 'The Secret Teachings of All Ages' by Manly Hall, pxc.)

Fact 5 - America was settled not only by the Pilgrim Fathers, but by luciferian Freemasons who established this country for a **peculiar and particular purpose known only to the initiated few** i.e. the sages, adepts and the elect. The purpose was to place Lucifer on the throne of the world. (See 'The Secret Teachings of All Ages' by Manly Hall, pxci.)

Fact 6 - The eye in the triangle on the reverse side of the U.S.$1 bill was originally the eye of Horus or Isis in Egyptian mythology but is now the eye of Lucifer, the god of Freemasonry. (See 'Morals and Dogma' by Albert Pike, p861.) The U.S. was therefore established to lead us into the New World Order. Read about the Palladium which is also known as the Cult of the Triangles. (See p23 of 'Better Than Nostradamus' by Barry Smith.)

Fact 7 - The Latin words on the left hand seal on the reverse side of the U.S.$1 bill when translated correctly read, **"Announcing the birth of a secular, heathenistic, ungodly New World Government (Religion, law system and economic system.)"** The Latin words on the ribbon in the beak of the bird, pictured in the right hand seal on the reverse side of the U.S.$1 bill translate as follows - **"Out of many, one."** In other words, the aim is to privatise all state owned enterprises and sell them out to overseas buyers who in turn can sell them to One World Government advocates. **"We are the World"** will be the key song sung in our lifetime. With our arms entwined, we will sway backwards and forwards in unison. We will leave behind our former nationalities as we will be known then as global citizens of planet earth. (See pg 75 of 'Better Than Nostradamus' by Barry Smith.)

Fact 8 - This luciferian concept has surreptitiously crept into some religious circles and other places of significance. (The eye in the triangle - see the Church of the Nativity in Bethlehem, the Church of the Annunciation in Nazareth and Hitler's Bunker at Eagle Nest.

15

See also p28 and p30 of 'Better Than Nostradamus' by Barry Smith.)

Fact 9 - The Freemasons' symbols of the compass and square are cleverly incorporated into the street map of Washington D.C. (See p68 of 'Better Than Nostradamus' by Barry Smith.)

Fact 10 - The Freemasons' Lodges have over 100 different degrees. Most Masons think there are only 33 degrees. (See p29 of 'Postscript' by Barry Smith.)

Fact 11 - The luciferian plan for World Government was called **New World Order** by George Bush in his pre-Gulf War speech and **Global 2000** by ex-U.S. President, Jimmy Carter. (See Internet - "President George Bush Announcing War Against Iraq".)

Fact 12 - There are many different groups involved in setting up this One World Government. George Bush referred to these satanically illumined groups in his pre-Gulf War speech as "1000 points of light".

Fact 13 - The law systems of the world must be weakened before the one world government is set up. A prophecy from the year 688B.C. makes this fact very clear. More sympathy for the perpetrator of the crime, than for the victim, is essential. *"Therefore the law is slacked, and judgment doth never go forth, for the wicked doth compass about the righteous, therefore wrong judgment proceedeth."*[4] e.g. The Lindy Chamberlain dingo case in Australia. (See p65 of 'Second Warning' by Barry Smith.) The sinking of a Russian liner in New Zealand waters. (See p177 of 'Final Notice' by Barry Smith.) The murders of President Kennedy, the U.S. citizens at the Branch Davidian Headquarters at Waco, Texas and the Oklahoma bombing. (See p1 of 'Better Than Nostradamus' by Barry Smith.)

Fact 14 - The plan to set up a secular, godless world government is doomed to failure. The prophet called it a 'vain thing'. *"Why do the heathen rage and the people imagine a vain thing? The kings of the earth set themselves, and the rulers take counsel together* *against the Lord, and against His Annointed saying, Let us break their bands asunder and cast away their cords from us."*[5]

A Simple Translation of the Above

World leaders gather regularly for official meetings yet well out of the public eye, conspirators from George Bush's 1000 Points of Light groups also meet for their new world government meetings at such places as Davos, Switzerland. The reasons for barring entrance to the press or photographers is easy to see.

These people plan to bring in a new world government without Christian or Judaic principles of morality. The key word, taken from the seal on the reverse side of the U.S.$1 bill, must be **seclorum** which means 'secular' or the 'absence of God'. This is to introduce Weishaupt's age of reason and the dumping of any beliefs in God as stuffy and outmoded.

The arrogant rascals held a so-called Wilderness Conference in Denver, Colorado, some years ago. I have a tape from that meeting where one of the participants states, **"We must keep this information from the cannon fodder that unfortunately populates the earth."** He was referring to people like you and me!

What Does God Think About All This?

Does He, as some imagine, sit in Heaven biting His heavenly fingernails? Not at all! *"He that sitteth in the Heavens shall laugh. The Lord shall have them in derision."*[6]

Another Simple Translation of the Above

Do you remember the seal on the right hand side of the reverse side of the U.S.$1 bill? The so-called American bald eagle is not an eagle at all. Let us see what Manly Hall, the top Freemasonry writer, has to say about this bird. *"Careful analysis of the seal discloses a mass of occult and masonic symbols, chief among them, the so-called American eagle...only the student of symbolism can see through the **subterfuge** and realise that **the American eagle upon the Great Seal is but a conventionalised phoenix**...."*[7] End quote.

17

Now, what is a phoenix? It's a mystical bird, prominent in Egyptian mythology. It burns in a fire, then sits upon its nest of flames until it can rise from its own ashes at a later date. Man's first attempt to thwart Almighty God's plans for the world, and set up his own global government was called the Tower of Babel. God smashed it![8]

Be very sure of this. The same God who smashed the Tower of Babel will also smash this modern day New World Order!

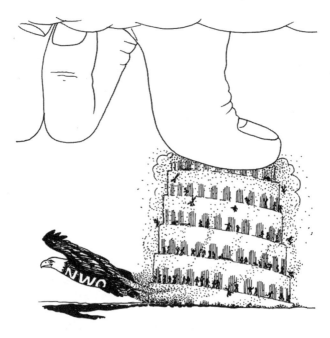

---

[1]II Thessalonians 2:6-7
[2]Revelation 13:16-18
[3]Revelation 12:12
[4]Habakkuk 1:4
[5]Psalm 2:1-3
[6]Psalm 2:4
[7]"The Secret Teachings of All Ages" by Manly Hall, pxc
[8]Genesis 11:1-9

Chapter Five
The Phoenix is Flying Again

George Bush called the plan, New World Order. Jimmy Carter called it Global 2000, which means that by the end of 1999, an organised crisis will get rid of the old and introduce the new. Little wonder that the whole plan makes God **laugh**. It goes without saying that not only does it cause Him amusement but also **derision** - *"to scorn, ridicule, too insignificant for serious consideration"* (Oxford Dictionary, p217).

Using very simple English, we see what God says about the New World Order and its surreptitious planners. *"You guys can't be serious. I, who inhabit eternity with no beginning or end of days, create all things for my pleasure, to operate as I designed them. Then along come a group of individuals who may live to the age of 80 years, if they look after themselves, who listen to the outrageous lies of Lucifer, otherwise known as Satan. Can you believe this? They hold what they consider to be secret meetings, not realising that I eavesdrop every time. They have the same aim as the builders of the Tower of Babel, to take over command from me. I hereby make the following declaration. All your carefully formed plans will come to nought. Your secret meetings held in Davos, Switzerland and other venues have been in vain. I, the same God who smashed the Tower of Babel, will also smash your Global 2000 New World Order. Please, I implore you, created beings, to* ***read a copy of my text book for life (the Bible). Read it and come to know Me, the Author!"***

Precis of the Luciferian Plan

In a devious and subtle manner, remove the assets from each country and thence the power and authority to govern and make their own decisions from governments world-wide. Set up a whole **network of think-tanks and advisors** who will all push the same party line and deceive the politicians from each individual country. Lend each country masses of money at very low interest rates, until they are completely trapped in an economic spider's web. Whilst their greedy little minds are working overtime as to how they can skim off some of this profit on the side for both themselves and their cronies in big business, make the head politicians sign conditions that ultimately they will see as being a clever trap, once the initial euphoria of receiving all that money has worn off.

Warning

Eastern countries are different **and smart**! They do not borrow money freely from international groups such as the Bank for International Settlements, or the G8 groups such as the IMF or the World Bank. These people love their **sovereignty** too much, and business-wise, they keep the business in the family for generation after generation.

They do not allow outside investors a finger in their business pie, therefore, they are not willing to freely **borrow and sign conditions** unless forced to do so.

A **scandal**, once fed to the news media, will do the trick however! e.g. *"Head of Hashimoto Bank Grants Illegal Loans to Cronies."* The result? Within a period of 24 hours, investors engage in taking their funds elsewhere. This is called "capital flight". The IMF, smiling in the wings, and licking their lips at the prospect of moving in on sovereign eastern countries, can hardly contain their glee. The trick appears to be working when suddenly, one man becomes a thorn in their flesh.

Prime Minister Mahathir from Malaysia

This man did what few others have had the intestinal fortitude to do - He called the IMF's bluff. Halfway through the month of June 1999, I was in Malaysia conducting seminars on these subjects. The audience stood and gave a standing ovation when I made the following statement - "Two countries not caught in the IMF trap are Singapore and Malaysia. Your Prime Minister Mahathir has resisted the efforts of the IMF to steal the sovereignty of your country. He is hated by world government forces and therefore cannot long remain in power. They will see to it that he soon goes, by hook or by crook."

Let us see what Dr Mahathir has to say. 'New Straits Times', 12th June 1999 - *"Don't resist globalisation but try to influence its process. The issue today is whether we should be globalised or not. Malaysian Prime Minister Datuk Seri Mahathir Mohamed recently expressed some doubts about globalisation....*

What does free trade really mean?

To most, it basically means that countries must reduce their trade barriers and open up their markets. **As the playing field is never even, the strong will always be at an advantage over the weak**." (Author's note - Adam Smith knew this. The whole plan is based on this 18th century Scottish economist's philosophies. Only one leader, Dr Mahathir has picked up on this vital point. Adam Smith called it survival of the fittest. Thus suicides borne out of despair, are irrelevant to this man and his demonic philosophies.)

Continue quote - *"The economic crisis has forced open the financial sectors of a number of affected countries **especially those that are obliged to the IMF**. Malaysia is fortunate in that it can still protect its financial market....*

It seems that globalisation is akin to an ideology of the powers that be. *Unlike the many isms that make up the known ideologies such as capitalism and communism, globalisation is less clear and even less dogmatic."* (Author's note - The New World Order catch phrase for this is **"The Third Way"**.)

Continue quote - *"....There is some sense of helplessness....Do you resist globalisation, or do you follow the adage; "If you can't beat them, join them"?*

...We are certainly not alone in expressing our reservations on globalisation..." End quote.

To you, Dr Mahathir, I endorse your sentiments. You are not alone!

Now, notice a further extension on this subject.

'Australian', 25th August 1999 - *"Mahathir woos China for a partner.*

Malaysian Prime Minister Mahathir Mohamed, has accorded no other nation the attention he lavished on China during a visit there last week.

....Dr Mahathir said China and Malaysia, together with

their neighbours, should look at how they could realise the Asian Monetary Fund, proposed by Japan and shot down by the United States and the International Monetary Fund...

If there had been such a body, Thailand, Indonesia and South Korea would not have needed to turn to the I.M.F....." End quote.

Excuse me - is anybody listening? (Please circle the appropriate word.)

Yes   No

If you circled the 'No', please shut the book and give it to someone else to read.

Chapter Six
Now for a Recap on the Plan

Using little known New Zealand as a test case, send IMF representatives to visit the Holyoake government in the year 1961.

1.   Lend them masses of money.
2.   The conditions must be signed at this point.
3.   Sit back and wait for 26 years until 1987.
4.   Find 5 men in the Labour Party of the day to listen to the ramblings of a Free Market philosopher called Adam Smith, whose ideas were picked up by a) The Adam Smith Institute and b) The Mont Pelerin Society, both based in London. Please look for both these groups on the Internet.

Using a private club of influential businessmen, some with links to the Mont Pelerin Society, go along with the plan to sell out the sovereignty of the country little by little. Thus, the government of the day, and I say this in the kindest possible way, become a **puppet** on a string, manipulated by the New Zealand Business Round Table.

Catch-words and catch-phrases appear regularly in the media which leave us all shaking our heads and asking for meanings e.g. **'There is some belt-tightening to be done'. 'There is some pain to be endured'**. The proverbial playing field is often mentioned and then on to the list of heavy words, dictated to the then Minister of Finance from his (be kind now) "advisors".

> 'Restructuring' - Sack thousands of workers. Choose six government departments to
> sell.
> 'Corporatisation' - Gradualism is the key word. Give these ex-government
> departments the hint that they will soon be controlled by businessmen and not
> politicians.
> 'Privatisation' - This clarifies the issue. The corporations are now going private.

As the ultimate aim of the exercise is to sell away your sovereignty overseas, the next catch-word must be 'Shares at 49% then increase those shares to 51% overseas and your government asset has gone forever.

Next, pay back some of your loans to the IMF. This leaves the government ultimately with **no money and no assets** with which to make money. From there, call in investors who are absolutely necessary to prop the country up and to stop it from collapsing.

Then try to introduce such scandalous bills as **MAI - Multilateral Agreement on Investment**, which would mean that overseas investors are given the freedom to come into one's country and snap up any further bargains. Not only that, they are given preference over local investors. It is quite disgusting really, and a blatant act of treasonous behaviour to even allow such a bill to see the light of day.

A coalition government is the final straw that breaks the camel's back. New Zealand called their system MMP (Mixed Member Proportional) whilst Tony Blair and various politicians in both Australia and the U.S.A. are using another term, which finishes up with the same result.

The Third Way or P.R. - Proportional Representation

The idea presented is that the old 2 party system is irrelevant.

The result of any **coalition is a weakened form of government** with many smaller parties voicing their ridiculous ideas and refusing to go along with the majority on any really sensible decision e.g. Italy, Israel and New Zealand - PDA = Political Disaster Areas.

Chapter Seven
The Lunatics Take Over

Oxford Dictionary 1988 - "**Lunatic** - An insane person. One who is extremely foolish or reckless".

A very revealing article in the 'New Citizen Mental Health Bulletin', http://www.cecaust.com.au - August/September 1998, will help us in our understanding. We quote in part - *"In 1984, a Labour government took power in New Zealand. Under the dictates of the British Crown's Mont Pelerin Society, it initiated what has been touted as "**the most fundamental free market revolution in the western world.**"*

*...Though begun by Labour, **lunatics** of all parties have intensified the "**reforms**".* (Break quote - Author's note - **Reforms are not about improving efficiency, but the selling up of sovereignty and independence.**)

Continue quote - *"...The developments cited here are some brief updates, some of them tragic, all of them crazy, on what New Zealand **inmates** have done since then.*

Not withstanding that New Zealand has the highest youth suicide rate in the world, spending on mental health has been slashed ruthlessly, seriously ill people walk the streets, or have to be tied up in their own homes for hours a day, to prevent them from injuring themselves or others. The rate of usage for Prozac (prescribed for depression) has tripled in the last year.

The government has announced a major police inquiry aimed at cutting funding and staff, and privatising many police functions. Already, police have to call the emergency 111 line for backup, because they have no money for radios. Police have started advising citizens, if attacked or burglarised, to call their neighbour first, then 111 because no one may answer at the latter. The Treasury-backed "review" is expected to result in hundreds more police officers being fired.

*The country's biggest city, Auckland, not only lost all electric power for two months recently (in its central business district) but after the lights finally came back in April, they went out again in early May, a situation which is expected to leave the city "vulnerable" to further blackouts for the next several weeks. The government announced an "inquiry into the blackout, but **specified the "inquiry" may not examine whether privatisation, (with its savage cuts in maintenance and staff) is what caused the problem in the first place."***

(Break quote - Author's note - Fascinating, fascinating. Imagine a murder investigation where the court sets limits. If the victim was killed by a bullet in the brain, the court does not wish to hear about it.)

. *"...The government recently floated **plans to privatise all roads**. Only a fierce public outcry, and charges that this was going back to the "Middle Ages" has caused the policy to be put temporarily on hold.*

A vicious work force plan is to be initiated, under which all those who receive sick-leave or disability payments are to be "tested" for their ability to perform work.

It has often been argued, that Mont Pelerin free market reforms wreak more havoc on a nation than a bombing campaign.

No wonder then, that Iraqi refugees from "Desert Storm" told an Auckland newspaper that they wanted to leave the country because "New Zealand is a terrible place to live". End quote.

The writer of this article, Mr Allen Douglas, has written a great deal more on this subject, and this is essential reading for any seeking the truth regarding Mont Pelerin's role in this attack on New Zealand before moving on to capture the rest of the world.

Away back on the 16th December 1991, Issue no.50, the 'Time' magazine produced an article on the results of these so-called "reforms". We quote in part - *"90 years ago the British Prime Minister described New Zealand as a **laboratory** for the instruction of older countries...*

"Many people have lost both hope and patience", says an unemployed factory worker...of Auckland. "People have taken such a hiding in this country, they'll just flop over and accept whatever is done to them.

*...The outcome of the **New Zealand experiment** is being closely watched by countries **like Australia and Canada, which have tentatively set out to restructure their economies on similar lines...***

...The man in charge of the Salvation Army Social Services programme in Auckland has no doubt, the recession is the worst since the 1930's. "We now have a level of poverty previously unthinkable in New Zealand", he says.

....Headmaster...asks his teachers to keep a special eye out for children who look faint, because they have come to school without eating.

...A top unionist says most people who are made redundant receive no compensation and in some cases, don't even get their leave entitlement. "Some of these people", he says, "are turning to crime."

...The founder of a new political party says, "People don't rob homes for t.v.'s and videos any more, they go for food and blankets.

*...**This decidedly assertive little country of 3.4 million people are wondering whether their leaders have taken them all on a national bungy leap without a safety harness.***

...The economic restructuring began with almost evangeli-cal zeal by former Labour Finance Minister, Roger Douglas....The elderly people, calling themselves "Grey Power", are shouting thirteen months later, "The good times seem no closer - how come? Seven years later, we're worse off than when all this started..."
End quote.

'Marlborough Express', 17th November 1998 - *"Reform fatigue sets in and the government is worried...It simply means the country is weary of living in ever changing times...**that change is often driven by ideology rather than sound practicality and usu-ally doesn't work...***

*Health is a prime example. Those with political memories that go back to 1991 will recall Simon Upton's grand plan for four separate health funding organisations and the inception of the **ghastly term 'crown health enterprises'**..."* End quote.

Actually, it was not Simon Upton but his friends in the London-based Mont Pelerin Society who dreamed up those murder-ous policies.

Okay. We have made this as clear as we can. If New Zealand was the **world's laboratory** in 1987, and a terrible experi-ment was conducted upon its unsuspecting citizens, what other horrible policies have been heaped upon it since that time.

To Citizens of Other Countries

Make up a check list, and record how these same policies have hit your country.
If they haven't arrived at your door yet, keep looking - **they will** (but always under a different name e.g. In New Zealand, we have **'restructuring'**. In South Africa it is called **'structural readjust-ment'**, Zimbabwe has **'economic structural adjustment pro-gramme'** (ESAP), and Zambia's is **'structural adjustment pro-gramme'** (SAP).

The hotel owner, deeply upset, publicly threatened to sue him unless he retracted his remarks.

Bob Hope promptly apologised and said, "I wish to say that I am sorry for my initial criticism re my board and lodgings. The rats that walked over me all through the night were not wearing hob-nailed boots."

Conspiracy Reality

From this simple illustration, we learn never to be so mentally structured that we automatically link the word **theory** with the word **conspiracy**. From this point on, by exercising your God-given intellect, you may delete the word **theory** from this conspiracy.

The world government advocates have many players which George Bush, in his pre-Gulf War speech, referred to as **"1000 points of light"**. Listeners to this information often ask the question - "You keep referring to 'they' - who are they?"

Read the next chapter and find out.

Chapter Nine
Let's Identify "Them"

Mr Bush's 1000 points of light mostly work within the sphere of their own interest group and in most cases are probably unaware of the other 999 group's activities. This information is "old hat" to many, yet to others, is enough to send a cold shiver up one's spine.

Please do not lump these people all together and put them in one labelled box - **"crazies"**. Be careful to recognise that you can only understand world events in proportion to your knowledge of:

a.   Who is organising these events?
b.   What they are really doing once all the wrapping has been stripped off?
c.   Why they are doing what they are doing?
d.   What will be the end result of what they are doing?

Here are the Names of Some of the Players

a.   The Council on Foreign Relations
b.   The Bilderbergers
c.   The Tri-Lateral Commission
d.   The Club of Rome
e.   The Bank for International Settlements
f.   The World Bank
g.   The G8
h.   The IMF
i.   Think-tanks world-wide
j.   The Adam Smith Institute
k.   The Mont Pelerin Society
l.   The Business Round Table
m.   The Centre for Independent Studies
n.   The Rothschilds family
o.   The Rockefeller family
p.   The Skull and Bones
q.   The Freemasons

These groups have powerful persons called "the shakers and the movers". Whilst some enjoy the fun and fellowship their society provides, some of the others have more sinister motives for belonging. Their aim is quite simple - **To change the world by getting rid of nation states and selling up the sovereignty and independence of each country until a new global governing force takes over.**

Q.   "How do you know?" I hear you ask.
A.   Because my country, New Zealand, was chosen to be the test case for the whole world!

Q.   How come the Newstalk ZB talkback host and others like him don't know all this? They live in New Zealand too, don't they?
A.   Yes, they do live in New Zealand but instead of doing some serious research in order to totally deny or confirm this conspiracy, they **prattle** on each night and their listeners **prattle** back to them, and they seldom learn anything new. Their listeners seldom know a lot more than the host, and so in their ignorance they feed each other and anyone who has the temerity to call in and state something different, is often promptly demolished by the host or an avalanche of phone calls from the listeners. Sad really.

Many years ago, Almighty God cried out in anguish through on of His prophets - *"My people are destroyed through lack of knowledge..."*[1]

Q.   How did these world government conspirators trap the sovereign country of New Zealand into becoming a laboratory or a test case?
A.   We will explain the answer to this question in the next chapter.

---

[1]Hosea 4:6

Chapter Ten
N.Z. Innocently Borrowed Some Money

If you wish to put somebody in your debt, lend them some money.

The wisest man who ever lived wrote this classic statement around the year 970 BC. *"The rich ruleth over the poor, and the borrower is servant to the lender."*[1]

The New Zealand guinea pig country took the bait in 1961. This country had full employment up until that point. The world government agents came to visit in the form of the International Monetary Fund (IMF). The then Prime Minister, Sir Keith Holyoake, fell for the **scam**. At that point, the count-down began.

A.   He borrowed the money at low interest rates, and lent it out to all and sundry. Farmers, rolling in their newly found affluence carried hay bales on the back seats of their BMWs and Daimler motorcars.

B.   Unfortunately, the Holyoake government officials also signed the **conditions**. To fool the people, long meaningless words and phrases must be employed. Thus, the conditions became **conditionalities policies** in New World Order jargon.

C.   The stage was now set for plan 3. By using the conditions imposed on New Zealand as their lever, the world government people (in the form of the IMF), **like a patient spider**, waited in their loan's web for 26 years. Meanwhile, **New Zealand (the fly)** borrowed more and more until they were hopelessly entangled.

In 1987, the world government spider slowly moved towards the fly.

The spider had lent the money and the fly had signed the conditions. **All that remained now was for the spider to suck the life force out of the fly.**

In simple English, 1987 was the year chosen by the New World Order leaders to conduct their experiment on poor little New Zealand. **The people never knew what hit them!** Gradually, their sovereignty and independence was stripped away. Their assets were sold, in many cases at **'mate's rates'**, to their cronies, and still the average citizen couldn't see it. They simply thought that it was new governmental policy. They were completely unaware of the conspiratorial nature of the so-called **'reforms'**.

As we have pointed out, even those who should know, don't. I am writing this in March 1999 and oh dear, I recently heard a man whom I had previously considered quite intelligent, say, **"I don't believe in conspiracy theories."**

As the Cockney may say to show his incredulity, "Cor, luv a duck!"

---

[1]Proverbs 22:7

Chapter Eleven
Proof of a Conspiracy

What you are about to read is so mind-boggling, that it could well become a feature programme in a popular t.v. series entitled "Previously Unsolved Mysteries." We could now go happily to the highest court in the land and prove our case.

Read Slowly and Carefully

British people understand the term - **Thatcherism**. Older Americans would probably be familiar with the term - **Reaganomics**. Folk from Alberta, Canada, with the term **Ralphonomics** and the majority of New Zealanders with the term - **Rogernomics**.

The 4th Labour Government in New Zealand came to power in 1984. They introduced their budget which gave New Zealanders little idea as to what they were in for. Their plans to fulfill the IMF conditions, were not told to the Labour Party members.

Proof - Rogernomics Kept Secret from the Party

'Press', 26th June 1987 - *"The Labour Party kept Rogernomics **secret** from party members before the 1984 General Election, the Prime Minister, Mr Lange, has told Australian television.*

...Mr Lange admits that Rogernomics would never have been implemented had it first been shown to party members, the "Auckland Star" reported.

*Mr Lange said "Labour's economic policy had to be sold to the party and the country in **various disguises**", the newspaper said."* End quote.

A Breakdown in Simple English

1. Had the Labour Party known beforehand about Rogernomics, they would have disallowed it.

2. Thus, a small group of politicians deliberately deceived their own political party members.

3. This same group of politicians deliberately deceived the voters of New Zealand.

4. The new economic policy was in reality **a deception**. It was not what the Labour Party or the voters thought it was.

5. The Concise English Dictionary interprets the word "disguise" as **"intended to deceive"**.

6. Thus, we may now deduce that the aim of the exercise was for these political persons, as yet un-named, to deceive two groups.

   a. Members of their party, many of whom elected them to their positions of leadership.

   b. The voters of New Zealand who elected them to Parliament in the first place.

Notice

The concise English dictionary gives us this definition of a **conspiracy** - "a plot, a treasonable combination."

If the above six points do not point to a conspiracy, then I'll eat this manuscript.

But wait, there's more.....

The Mystery Men Revealed

Later, another New Zealand publication assisted us with the task of establishing whether or not, this was a true conspiracy foisted on New Zealand from 1984 onwards.

(In previous books written on these subjects, I deliberately omitted full names of participants for one good reason. These people, I have no doubt at all, were absolutely sincere in all their secrecy, disguises and the like. They all had their own world view, and this, in fairness and justice, is their right. However, since the plot is so serious, and they are committed to it - and presumably will be happy to hold to their beliefs if exposed - I have decided to use their names in full. Of course, non-New Zealand readers will probably not recognise any of these characters.)

The Plan

The 'Listener', 19th December 1987 - *"By piecing together the statements and documents, it can be shown that "Rogernomics" was a plan imposed by a small group of ministers on a party which had confused ideas as to what it was letting itself in for. Ultimately, the Lange, Palmer, Caygill, Prebble, Douglas view of the economic policy had been endorsed before the snap election...Even the Prime Minister, David Lange, acknowledged that the agenda of Rogernomics had been withheld from the party which had campaigned for his election."* End quote.

Breakdown in Simple English

This article, presented in a reputable N.Z. publication tells us the following:

a.   Five men are named.

b.   Their devious plan was arranged and agreed upon before the election in 1984.

c.   The Labour Party at the time didn't really understand what the repercussions of this plan were as they were **'confused'**.

d.   Once again, we see that the plan included in Rogernomics was **not** clearly explained to other party members before it was implemented.

It looks to be akin to a **conspiracy** to me but there again, my grasp on the English language, my mother tongue, may be lacking. Maybe all these points put together still does not represent a conspiracy theory to some determined doubters.

But that's not all....

Why Did They Choose New Zealand?

Well, they initially gave it a try with Margaret Thatcher from Great Britain but the whole things went down like a lead balloon. Margaret tried to save herself politically by conducting a ridiculous little war in the Falkland Islands but instead of boosting her popularity in the polls, it left a lot of dead soldiers on both sides, masses of grieving families and dear Margaret received the D.C.M.[1] for her efforts.

In the late 1980's, the President of the World Bank visited New Zealand. Read carefully what he said. *"New Zealand's economic restructuring was a ROLE MODEL for other countries which also had to adjust their policies to achieve growth,"* the World Bank President, Mr Barber Conable, said.
*At a press conference after talks with the Minister of Finance, Roger Douglas, and the Prime Minister, David Lange, Mr Conable said, "The policies **wisely pursued in New Zealand had not been without pain** but were now showing benefits in an improving economy."* End quote.

He forgot to add, **"and larger bank balances for all who assisted in selling up or buying New Zealand's assets."**

New Zealand - Where's That?

I tell you this place is so out of the way, very few know exactly how to describe its position on the map. During one visit to the U.S.A., I asked a whole classroom full of children where New Zealand was. The closest anyone got was to say it was part of Australia.

Many patriotic New Zealanders feel that their country is important on the world stage but even at this late stage, they still have not come to the realisation that their country was chosen, pre 1984, as a **laboratory, a test case, or guinea pig** to try out an **audacious, outrageous, experiment**. Under this treatment, the whole country would be torn apart, government assets would be sold, in many cases, very cheaply to friends or cronies, and the national debt would sky-rocket, as would the country's suicide rate.

Q.   Did the perpetrators understand what they were doing and the end results of it all?
A.   Some obviously did. Some didn't.

Q.   How can you be so positive with your answer?
A.   Because it was answered for us by one of the politicians in power, when the Rogernomics plan was put into operation.

Proof Once Again

On the 20th of December, 1997, the Prime Minister of New Zealand, Mr David Lange, who was in power when Rogernomics started, was interviewed by Brian Edwards on the programme called 'Top of the Morning'. Please keep in mind two key dates -

1984 - Labour Party comes to power. Introduces new budget.
1987 - The implementation of the IMF wrecking conditionalities policies - conditions.

"Q.   *When you were elected in 1984, did you know what you were going to do?*
A.   ***We implemented policies we did not recognise. Traditional Labour voters felt they had been betrayed!!*****"
End quote.

Echo:
"We implemented policies we did not recognise."
"We implemented policies we did not recognise."
"We implemented policies we did not recognise."

Hello, hello, hello. What is happening to the term "**conspiracy theory**".

Some of these men had studied the policies carefully and were thoroughly committed to pressing on, even if it looked like political suicide e.g. Roger Douglas and Richard Prebble. These two regularly worked together and occasionally still do even to this day (late 1999). Some of the others went along for the ride, possibly not initially understanding the terrible long-term effects of these policies e.g. David Lange.

It was for this reason that part-way through the Rogernomics so-called reforms, (what a misnomer), the Prime Minister, who was brought up in a Godly, Christian home, saw clearly, with his own eyes, the suicides, the social wreckage of his country, and endeavoured to halt the plan. He sacked his Minister of Finance. It was too late. The Minister of Finance, then others after him, like a runaway horse with the bit between his teeth, had followed the ideas of a Roman general, Fabius, upon which Fabian Socialism was founded. 'Move gradually at first - then hit hard and never deviate, otherwise all the waiting has been in vain.'

I myself heard the Prime Minister say words along this line, "Roger, the plan is killing me." He couldn't sleep, nor rest as he obviously loved New Zealand and its people.

A Number of Questions are in Order

Q.   If the so-called reforms were not thought up by any of those 5 men, where did they come from?

Q.   Why did they have the audacity to call these innovations to society **'reforms'** (to make better)?

The only people who could possibly think that life is better in New Zealand than it was pre-1987 are:

a.   Those who made a financial killing out of buying up government assets at mates' rates.

b.   Some of those residing in psychiatric hospitals.

c.   Those overseas people who read the glowing, lying, reports about New Zealand's successful reforms, in many cases no doubt written by the perpetrators and passed on to their sympathetic cronies in the media world.

The same system was used in the U.S.A. to keep Bill Clinton in power during 1998-1999. False media polls were conducted giving the impression that the vast majority wished him to stay in power. This would of necessity imply that the citizens of that country are a bunch of reprobates like their commander in chief. It may be of interest to note that well over 50 people associated with the Clintons are now deceased. I doubt whether any of those people, or their families who remain on earth, would wish Bill to remain as president. I feel that they probably have other plans for him.

The reality is that these results were simply not true, just as it is in no way true that New Zealand is better off now than it was before.

Q.   **What sort of a fool would sell his house to pay the rates?**
Who planned all this nonsense anyway?

---

[1]Don't Come Monday

Chapter Twelve
Think Tanks Named -
The Adam Smith Institute (ASI)
The Mont Pelerin Society (MPS)
Centre for Independent Studies (CIS)

These three groups are but a small number of societies called "**think tanks**". Some of George Bush's **1000 points of light.**

Politicians are generally drawn from the main stream of society and have two qualities that help them get their jobs.

A.   The **'gift of the gab'** - good talkers.
B.   **Financial backers** in the form of big business. They all have plenty of **advisors** in whom they desperately wish to t rust.

The bottom line is simply this. The member of Parliament soon finds out, upon entering the hallowed halls of Parliament, that good ideas he or she may have are better kept to themselves. (This is why many under MMP simply resign and go back to normal employment. They can't stand the **lies and deception along with the intrigue**.)

Real danger comes at this point. If a person connected to big business is a financial backer of a political party and also a member of a think tank, the poor figurehead politician becomes almost irrelevant or simply a "yes" man. **If you are a politician and say "no", you are down the road very swiftly indeed.**

Proof, Proof, I Hear You Cry!

Come on, please! Let us be quite frank about all this. The three groups named at the beginning of this chapter i.e. ASI, MPS and CIS, are virtually unknown to the vast majority of people. Yet, my dear reader, it is the policies of these people that are influencing your life at this moment, even as you read this page.

"I don't care a straw", I hear someone say. You will by the end of this year, 1999, when the Y2K millennium bug begins to bite!

Q. How did you first hear about the existence of these three groups?

A. A newspaper article was sent to me at the right time. I needed it!

Reforms Cited as Example

'Waikato Times', 20th March 1996 - ***"The influential Adam Smith Institute has urged Britain to emulate New Zealand's public sector reforms*** *in a report just released.*

The think-tank named after the 18th century free-market economist will also be addressed on the reforms by former Finance Minister, Sir Roger Douglas, at a meeting in Westminster on Friday (N.Z. time).

*...The Adam Smith Institute largely credits David Lange's Labour Government for the changes which have led to New Zealand's balanced Budget (**lies**) and faster economic growth (**lies**), lower inflation and lower income tax than Britain.*

...They recommend that Britain should follow New Zealand's example, and make the Bank of England independent, with the governor made personally responsible for hitting a low inflation target.

*In the last decade, **New Zealand has been the world's laboratory for public sector reform (truth)**...If our politicians - from whichever party - want to know how to change Britain for good, they need merely to book a flight to Auckland...."* End quote. (The words **'lies' and 'truth'** has been inserted by this author.) Actually, our parliamentarians meet in Wellington.

Excuse me. Do you feel that we could be on the right track? (Please circle the appropriate word.)

Yes   No

If you circled the 'No', please stop reading at this point and watch a programme on television instead.

Chapter Thirteen
Challenge to the Sceptics

During a lecture tour in 1998, I spoke to a crowd of people night by night at the City Temple, London. Recognising the fact that some of the listeners found the information we presented so **'way out'** that they had trouble believing any of it was true, we presented them with some Internet addresses to start them off on their path to find the truth.

We told them to hook up to the Internet and look up:
The Adam Smith Institute - http://www.adamsmithinstitute.com
The Mont Pelerin Society - http://www.cis.org.au/Policy/mps.html
Centre for International Studies - http://cis.org.au/

The next evening, I asked how many had accepted the challenge and looked up those web-sites. The hall was immediately charged with excitement. People called out **"It's true - it's true"**, then shouted and clapped.

Some Information on Each Group

ASI - A non-party organisation named after the 18th century Scots philosopher and economist, Adam Smith. Founded in Great Britain in 1978, it is based in London and it advises governments on such subjects as:

a. Privatisation
b. Contracting out government services to the private sector
c. Improving public services
d. National health service reforms
e. Independent Seminars on the open society
f. No state funds for political parties
g. Deregulation of Utilities e.g. Telecom
h. Transport for Tomorrow - new toll roads - sale of British Rail
i. Welfare state reform - cut out benefits (gradually of course)
j. Employee share ownership
k. Choice in education

l.   Privatising Scotland's ferries
m.   Privatising the London Underground
n.   Phasing out subsidies for farmers
o.   Liberalising Sunday trading

MPS - Fifty years ago, a small group of European and American intellectuals met at the Swiss village of Mont Pelerin to discuss the future of liberalism. The moving force behind the meeting was the Austrian-born, although by then, British economist, F.A. Hayek.

'Policy', Autumn 1967, "Threats to Freedom Then and Now" by Greg Lindsay.
"...What then is the Mont Pelerin Society, what did it set out to achieve, and has it been successful? Why would the 'Sunday Times', in an article on April 13, call it "**the most influential but little-known think-tank of the second half of the 20th century?**"
...In 1944, Hayek published his book, "The Road to Serfdom", dedicated to "socialists of all parties"...
...What was once a European and American club, now has members from all continents.
In the 1990's the New Zealand members are, Roger Kerr and Alan Gibbs, (both members of the Business Round Table) and a New Zealand parliamentarian, Simon Upton. The ex-Minister of Finance, Ruth Richardson and also Richard Prebble of the ACT party, also espouse Mont Pelerin concepts." End quote. (As did Roger Douglas, ex-Minister of Finance for New Zealand 1987.)

The MPS hold high-level policy training seminars for cabinet ministers and policy makers at a stately country house outside of London and their work is funded by international donors e.g. The Asian Development Bank and the World Bank etc etc.

Adam Smith was the father of privatisation and other 20th century ideas including the separation of private business and government. The government gradually phases out of running business and funding their various departments e.g. welfare, hospitals, schools, police, fire services etc. Private business groups subtly begin to take over this role.

He was not overly compassionate, and his "freemarket reform philosophies" in reality provided a platform for the **survival of the fittest**, by fair means or foul, and the pauperisation and possibly suicide of the dejected remainder.

As we may now see, his plans are working to a tee. Under the modern "freemarket reforms", the winner takes all and the previously employed, previously happy and contented loser is consigned to the proverbial scrap heap.

The catch phrase used in this case is another misnomer. It is called **"a level playing field"**. For some, however, it has proved to be more level than for others!

Chapter Fourteen
New Zealand

At this time of writing in January, 1999, what is the situation in the Illuminati laboratory country? The Labour Government of Prime Minister David Lange, came to power in 1984, and commenced their Mont Pelerin, Business Round Table shenanigans in earnest during 1987. What did that Prime Minister confess on radio ten years later?

"We implemented policies we didn't recognise..."

Neither did the man in the street!

All these new catchwords appeared regularly. (**Hey, don't you call me a "conspiracy nutter". You're reading about a real conspiracy right now!**)

1. Restructuring
2. Corporatisation
3. Privatisation
4. Share overseas at 49%
5. Shares overseas at 51%
6. Pay back the IMF
7. Result, no assets and no money left to operate government
8. Call in investors, mainly from South East Asia. In 1998, 80,000 Chinese lived in Auckland alone.
9. Immigration opens doors to wealthy foreigners. Without them, New Zealand goes down the economic tube.
10. Final indignity. Introduce a new system of government, following the German model.

Title - M.M.P. - Mixed Member Proportional. Meaning - masses of tiny parties all voicing their ideas which proves to be completely unworkable. The whole thing finally collapses, yet our **Illuminati bosses** require that we never return to the old proven system of two major parties.

A new lady Prime Minister is elected along with her National Party. She is smart. She sees that the MMP coalition cannot succeed. She **speaks vehemently against it,** and promises a referendum knowing that all New Zealanders with a brain will vote against it.

However, the plot thickens. At this stage, it becomes so obvious that I must make this portion of the story so clear that there can be no doubt.

Right at the end of January 1999, Jenny Shipley, the Prime Minister of New Zealand, flies off on a quick tour of three major countries.

1. The U.S.A. - She meets - can you believe it - naughty Bill right in the middle of his false impeachment trial.
2. Jenny and Tony Blair, ever smiling as usual, pictured together shaking hands for a long time, which, I believe, is the accepted custom.
3. From there to Germany.

Now, my conspiratorial friends and readers, whilst on this journey, she gets a word of advice in her pink little ear from some Illuminati character. Let's listen in for a moment.

"Jenny, if you wish to keep your job, we would recommend that upon your arrival back in New Zealand, you should make it very clear that you have changed your mind about MMP. You must let people know how successful it is in Germany and **although the New Zealand experience has been the biggest political botch up in history, you will continue on with it.**

You see, Jenny, we have told Tony Blair in Great Britain to bring the same system in to his country. However, to confuse the people over there, we have changed the name from MMP to PR. This stands for **Proportional Representation**. It will do the same job - destroy the political power base of Great Britain!"

When this diabolical plan was let loose on New Zealand from 1984-1987, an article from the "Listener" magazine helped us to understand who implemented it.

The Plan

'Listener', 19th December 1987 - *"By piecing together the statements and documents it can be shown that "Rogernomics" was a plan imposed by a small group of ministers which had confused ideas as to what it was letting itself in for. Ultimately, the Lange, Palmer, Caygill, Prebble, and Douglas view of the economic policy had been endorsed before the snap election. Even the Prime Minister David Lange, acknowledged that the agenda of Rogernomics had been withheld from the party which had campaigned for his election."* End quote.

Please note the following points. The Prime Minister of the day freely acknowledged that this weird agenda was initially hidden from the party of which he was the head. Ten years later, he acknowledges on public radio, **"We implemented policies we did not recognise."**

It gets worse!

We read in another publication, the Christchurch 'Press', 26th June 1987 - *"**Rogernomics kept secret from the party**.*

The Labour Party hierarchy kept Rogernomics secret from party members before the 1984 General Election, the Prime Minister Mr Lange, has told Australian television.

Mr Lange admits Rogernomics would never have been implemented had it first been shown to party members, the Auckland 'Star' reported.

Mr Lange said Labour's economic policy had to be sold to the party and the country in VARIOUS DISGUISES (emphasis added), the newspaper said." End quote.

New Zealand readers, remember at all times that your country was the **"laboratory"**, **"guinea pig"**experimental nation for all these Illuminati New World Order plans.

Read what Bill Clinton's mentor, hero and role model,

Quigley says, and then see how they conned New Zealand from 1987 onwards.

"The history of the last century shows that....**the advice given to governments by bankers** (who, as we have seen, control the governments) like the advice they gave to industrialists, was consistently **good for the bankers**, but often **disastrous for governments**, businessmen and people generally..." **Please note that this is not the claim of a "conspiracy theorist" but it is a plain statement of fact by a recognised insider**...." End quote.

What We Have Learned Thus Far

1.	There were five men in the New Zealand Labour Party's top echelon who **conspired** (and that's a powerful word) to introduce a brand new economic system to their country.
2.	They obviously didn't really understand what they were doing nor the repercussions of this plan as they had confused ideas as to what they were letting themselves in for. The reason for this confusion was that only once before in the history of the world had anybody else ever attempted to foist such a massive delusion on a population of thinking people. Margaret Thatcher tried it and received the D.C.M.[1]
3.	The Plan had been picked up by one of the five, who did too much reading of heavy books on the subject of economic theory late at night.
4.	Even before the Labour Party won the election, these five conspirators knew what they were going to do.
5.	These five men deliberately kept the plan from the rest of the Labour Party and the voters who elected them.

It was so far removed from Labour Party policy that the Prime Minister of the day, 10 years later, confessed on public radio that "traditional Labour voters felt they had been betrayed.

Remember what else he said in the same interview?

'Top of the Morning', 20th December 1997 - **"We implemented policies we did not recognise."**

51

6.   The Prime Minister of the day, a man with a social conscience, began to see what was happening and had a fall out with the then Minister of Finance. He made it clear that he was losing sleep over the whole deal but still the average New Zealander couldn't see what it was all about.

[1]Don't Come Monday

Chapter Fifteen
Other Countries Affected by the New Zealand Experience

Who Are These Other Countries?

Canada - During the month of May 1994, we conducted a lecture tour of Canada. The Premier of Alberta, Mr Ralph Klein, had just had a visit from New Zealand's ex-Minister of Finance, and the promoter of Rogernomics - Roger Douglas. Sure enough, Ralph took the restructuring story on board, hook, line and sinker. The media called the Alberta plan, **Ralphonomics.**

We read this warning written by a fellow New Zealander to the Canadians from the 'Edmonton Journal', 1st May 1994 - *"New Zealander warns of Deficit Cut Hoax....*

*Alberta faces economic disaster and the collapse of its social system if it continues following **a political 'hoax', imported from New Zealand**, warns a Labour leader from that country.*

*The speaker from New Zealand said the conservative **'confidence trick'** that deficits must be controlled at all costs had led her country of 3.5 million people to the brink of ruin...*

"When the programme started, the politicians used peoples' natural fear of debt to sell it", she said. "Debt was the threat. Economic restructuring was the salvation...."

*"But after ten years of massive change, **New Zealand's problems are worse than before**...."*

"The privatisation plan included a massive sell-off of twelve billion dollars in public assets which included a national airline, a railway, a telephone company and an oil company." End quote.

'Edmonton Journal', 21st May 1994 - *"Province asks churches to help victims of Klein's cuts."* End quote.

'Edmonton Journal', 19th May 1994 - *"Fear of job cuts causing terrible stress.*

During the French Revolution, many aristocrats never knew when they would face Madame Guillotine.

Today in budget cutting Edmonton, many workers don't know when they will face the axe and experts say that uncertainty is more stressful than the actual chop....Job loss can also lead to strained relationships, financial problems and more stress." End quote.

Canada follows New Zealand. Result? An absolute disaster!

Russia is another country visited and conned by Illuminati advisors including New Zealand's ex-Minister of Finance. By following the New Zealand model of the Illuminati restructuring plan introduced to Russia by Roger Douglas, the Mafia have taken over the economy.

New Zealand 'Herald', 20th February 1992 - *"The former Minister of Finance, Sir Roger Douglas, is off soon to talk to the Russians about privatisation...*
*Sir Roger said he would be part of a three man advisory committee organised by the **World Bank**...."* End quote.

The World Bank obviously is very fond of New Zealanders. A former New Zealand Prime Minister, Sir Robert Muldoon, was appointed as one of the 6 governors of this group, soon after losing his position in New Zealand politics. It can now be shown that this well-known New Zealand leader was also under the power of the Illuminati New World Order people. He actually confessed during the course of one of his speeches that New Zealand was following the G7 plan and yielding up measures of sovereignty.

'Sunday Star', 27th January 1987 - *"Mr Muldoon speaks about G7."*

In the article Mr Muldoon spoke of 45 representatives from different countries meeting in Rome. Quote - *"...to see what we could do to mobilise public opinion in our various sphere of influence to give political support to the difficult decisions that have to be taken by the governments of the G7 to implement the policies that are now seen to be necessary...*

...The G7 proposal involves some loss of sovereignty by the participants and that is where the political difficulty arises. If the public, or more correctly, the electorate of those countries, can be persuaded that the result of that loss of sovereignty is higher standards of living for all the people of the world, the political difficulty will be overcome." End quote.

'European', 31st August - 6th September 1995 - *"Russian Bank Crisis May Spark Return to Dictators.*
Economists in Russia say that the country's banking crisis is so severe that it could lead to a return to dictators." End quote.

'The Sunday Times', 13th September 1998 showed a photo-graph of a platoon of Russian soldiers walking in columns with cabbages under their arms. Their pay from the Russian government - cabbages!

Russia follows New Zealand. Result? An absolute disaster!

Australia. The Kiwi Experiment, the Aussie media called it.

'Australian', 1992, Ian Henderson, Economics Correspond-ent - *"New Zealand's robust approach to micro-economic reform has been held up as a model for this country. But research has cast doubt on whether the gain has been worth the pain.*
...Detailed analysis undertaken by a New Zealand econo-mist has concluded the country's growth performance has been the worst of any industrialised country for the past World War II period overall and the for the first eight years since the country's eco-nomic reforms begun in 1984." End quote.

Keating left the Prime Ministership and in came honest John Howard. Poor John. A good name to uphold, and he meets his new bosses, the Illuminati fronts i.e. The Business Council of Australia and others in the field of big business.

How is this for a headline? New Zealand 'Herald', 17th February 1997 - ***"Howard told to follow New Zealand.***

An influential Asian business journal has urged Prime Minister John Howard to be more radical and learn from New Zealand...." End quote.

During the course of 1997, his bosses tell him that his next job is to subdue the powerful MUA (Maritime Union of Australia) and then to sell up the remainder of the Australian telecommunications giant, Telstra. The Aussie citizens hate to see the money-making Telstra giant go but even though it looks like political suicide, we must do what the boss says, mustn't we?

Although obviously a man of integrity, to tell the electorate the truth, that he and his government are no longer running Australia, would earn him the sack. If he dared to use the word **'Illuminati'**, he may even get the bullet.

Following the New Zealand plan, they changed the names of their government departments. This helps add to feelings of despair and confusion e.g. **the Government Employment Agency now has a new name - Centrelink**.

Now, when you go through this lengthy experience of restructuring, (which really means that this is stage one of selling up to an overseas group), what is your first duty?

Why, sack thousands of people of course! And that's exactly what this crowd has done. Look!

The 'Australian', 5th November 1998 - *"Centrelink to slash staff by 6000.*
Centrelink were bracing themselves yesterday for more staff redundancies. About 6000 staff were expected to be offered packages to leave Centrelink in a move that would slash the size of the agency by more than a third since the coalition came to power...." End quote.

Q.   I used to wonder why so much money was offered in their packages. How could they possibly recoup all that they lost?

A.	Easy. **This is a "one off" action**. Once they're gone, they are gone forever. No more wage payouts. The recipients of the packages leave with smiles on their faces as they are temporarily happy with the cold hard cash in their hot, little hands. Later, however, if no others jobs are available, gloom sets in as they face the prospect of long term unemployment.

And again, from the same newspaper, *"Tide of Poverty Rises.*

Rising numbers of low income earners are being turned away from welfare organisations as the community sector struggles to cope with increased levels of poverty.
The disturbing findings form part of Australians Living on the Edge, a national survey of more than 500 frontline community agencies...many people are going away empty-handed...
The biggest issues facing the agencies were the impact in government policies..." End quote.

Author's note - Correction! These are not government policies. They are the Mont Pelerin Societies' policies.

G.S.T. for Australia

What a laugh! We have visited this country many times over the last twenty seven years. To us in New Zealand, it is simply a hop, skip and a jump to get there in approximately 3 hours by plane. Sometimes it is less expensive to go to Australia than to fly to the other end of New Zealand.

Some years ago, Prime Minister Paul Keating, said, "We are going to introduce a Consumption Tax. If we fail to implement it, I will resign". He failed to do implement it and he also failed to resign.

Some years later, another Aussie politician, a Dr Hewson, said, "Vote for me and I will introduce G.S.T. (Goods and Services Tax). This is similar to saying, **"Vote for me and I'll shoot you in the head"**. Not surprisingly the poor man missed out on becoming Prime Minister of Australia.

Not wishing to fail in following the Mont Pelerin Think Tank plan for a third time, the Prime Minister, John Howard, appeared to be committing **political suicide** as he once again brought the subject up.

Any Australian who understood the disastrous effect it had on New Zealand citizens immediately gave it the thumbs down. Mr Howard was most cunning as he tried to con the people using a psychological approach. Australians should take careful note in the future as he carefully avoided using the letters G.S.T. Instead he referred to it as 'taxation reform'. As the average Aussie has about the same level of intellect as the average Kiwi had when he was being sucked in, he listens with wonder as his Prime Minister, whom he desperately wants to trust, intones, "**The average little Aussie battler is longing for taxation reform.**"

Strange! I myself have walked the streets of many Australian cities, yet not once in all these years (27) have I ever heard a 'little Aussie battler' say, **"Oh, how I long for taxation reform!"**

Who is Giving the Aussies Advice on GST?

Why, the New Zealand Prime Minister who was in power when the Illuminati destruction plan and sell-out of New Zealand was initiated.

Christchurch 'Press', 30th August 1997 - *"The Australian Government should follow New Zealand's lead and introduce a goods and services tax (GST) without fanfare, says former New Zealand Prime Minister, David Lange.*

Mr Lange told ABC radio yesterday that his government did not even tell New Zealand residents that it was introducing a ten per cent GST in 1986, let alone promise it would be kept at the same rate.

"That's why it was so successful. We didn't talk about it for years. We did it. And we did it quickly enough for them to see the benefit of it so that more people wanted it than didn't..." Break quote.

Author's note - Oh dear, the article was going so well to this point, and amidst all the truth, we suddenly get hit with an outright lie. **Most New Zealanders hate GST!**

Continue quote - *"**With taxation like that, you've got to get your finger into their wallets without disturbing their trousers**...you don't sort of wave a flag and blow a bugle and say, "I'm now going to put this on..."* End quote.

O.K. Please make it quite clear in your mind that along with all other world leaders, John Howard is merely giving the illusion that he is running the country. A very sincere man, no doubt, but along with politicians world-wide, caught in the Illuminati trap!

Chapter Sixteen
Further Indignities Heaped On New Zealand

Christchurch 'Press', 28th September 1998 - *"GP's urged to tell on colleagues."*

Sunday 'Star Times', 28th December 1997 - *"Motorists dob in bad drivers."*

Christchurch 'Press', 28th October 1998 - *"Sick man denied urgent treatment."*

'Marlborough Express', 28th October 1998 - *"A growing number of mentally ill people are living on Christchurch streets."*

'Dominion', 15th January 1999 - *"....Not content with selling our financial sector to the Australians and our telecommunications and railway networks to the Americans, Mr Prebble now wishes to sell Contact Energy, TVNZ, N.Z. Post, the produce boards. ACT'S plans for local government also make it clear that the ownership of our town water supplies and roading networks will be simply remitted to the highest bidder.*

...In "ACT world" citizens will be required to surrender more and more of their autonomy to the unelected and largely unaccountable owners of private institutions.

...with radio, television, book publishing, and most of the newspapers in foreign hands, the term "New Zealand" will rapidly become a purely geographical expression...." End quote.

'Dominion', 14th December 1998 - "Thousands lose forestry jobs.

New Zealand 'Herald', 20th January 1998 - *"**Clustering:** the way ahead for New Zealand...*

Instead of growing standard grain crops, it would be simple to find niche markets for specialised grains.

"Nobody makes money today out of exporting commodities - be it logs, carcases of lambs or even teaching people the English language at the commodity end of education. We need to move into a high value-added differentiated stream of activity.

...In Professor Porter's words, we need to....create a sense of vision between industries which can work together and inspire the nation as a whole." End quote.

What challenging words and noble aspirations for a nation

that is still being ripped apart! What on earth is he talking about?
Please notice the brand new catch word of **'clustering'**.

    'Dominion', 18th December 1998 - *"Struggling farmers are being forced to pay up mortgages or sell their farms, despite many never having missed a loan payment....*

    New Zealand 'Herald', 4th May 1998 - "A bid for a controlling stake in Wellington International Airport has been made by the local subsidiary of Scottish transport company, Stagecoach..."

    New Zealand 'Herald', 4th May 1998 - "New Zealand has been able to create jobs at a faster rate than Australia, because of the Employments Contracts Act...

    The study comes as Canberra continues its attempt to bulldoze industrial reform against determined opposition..." End quote.

    Author's note - The Mont Pelerin advisors made this a key issue.
1.   Allay the workers' fears by calling the smashing of union power **"reforms"**.
2.   Using clever psychology, introduce an act of Parliament so cunningly phrased that the word **"unions"** is not even mentioned.

These people are playing for keeps and are devilishly cunning.

    By the way, can you believe how ignorant the majority of politicians are? As I pen these lines on the 2nd November 1999, just prior to the New Zealand elections, the Labour Party are trying to encourage the unions' voters that they intend to repeal the Employment Contracts Act. This was the Mont Pelerin plan that was used to smash the unions and bring in personal contracts. One must ask, "How desperate and stupid can one become in one's search for power?

'Sunday Star Times', 29th November 1998 - *"Suicide on the farm.*

    ...Seven farmers in the greater Manawatu region....have committed suicide this year, leaving behind a trail of bereaved friends and families, still asking "Why?" End quote.

    'EIR', 15th January 1999 - *"...While New Zealand's savage "free market" reforms far surpass even those of Margaret Thatcher and Tony Blair's Britain and have left the country in ruins, **the***

reforms have provided a small fortune for those who designed them - associates of the Mont Pelerin Society....

Gore's New Zealand model is also beloved of the International Monetary Fund (IMF) and World Bank, which have paid New Zealand politicians to fly all over the world to spread its **"free market poison"**, *including Germany, Russia, Brazil, Argentina, Mexico, Pakistan, Canada, Peru, Vietnam, South Africa, Singapore and Australia.*

*...In the 2nd half of 1996, a study of the New Zealand model was conducted...based on statistics from New Zealand government departments. The results, published in 1997 showed,....**the country's foreign debt sky-rocketed from NZ$16.359 billion in 1984 to more than $74 billion, despite the fact that debt-cutting was the chief proclaimed motivation for carrying out the reforms.*** " End quote. (Emphasis added.)

Did anybody ever apologise to the people of New Zealand, or confess that they had made a mistake? No, they didn't!

Christchurch 'Press', 24th October 1998 - "Change, before paradise is lost.

Like thousands of New Zealanders,.....I'd got the wanderlust out of my system and had done my bit for promoting New Zealand as a switched-on, progressive little place.

...Then I came home.

...The months passed and my feeling of being cheated grew. Many of the people in charge of New Zealand grew up in the same era as myself. They benefited from free, high quality education, health services, and a life-style envied almost everywhere.

Having had their slice of the cake, they are now systematically dismantling this system, and depriving the next generation of the same privileges they experienced.

...Questionable people in high-paid jobs receive pay rises following evidence they deceived us regarding their financial interests.

...What.....is going on in this country? How much more will people take before the revolution begins?

...For too long, politicians have been exploiting the apathy of New Zealanders and now they certainly appear to be on a roll.

Without doubt, the same politicians will blame everyone else and everything else for our predicament: global economic downturn, overseas import tariffs, and the like.

...Never have I seen such a bunch of impressionable fools as my countrymen.

Too many of us believe we still live in a clean, green, go ahead, little place which people the world over are dying to live in. Sadly, if they come here and fall ill, at the wrong end of the country, they may do just that.

The reality is, we are allowing the powers that be to rob us of health care, education and essential services. ***Anything remaining is being sold off to the highest bidder for no other reason that we can be seen as progressive and trend-setting in the world economic circle.***

...We, the so-called ordinary people sit on the sidelines and watch our country slide even further from its vaunted position in the world's social hierarchy. Soon, we will look back and remember Paradise Lost." End quote.

It just goes on and on. Poor little guinea pig New Zealand. If it's new, and no-one else wants it, send it to New Zealand!

Rotten petrol - Some time ago, someone brewed up a bad batch of gasoline. Where did they send it? New Zealand, of course. A close friend, Nic Venter, who does the art work for these books, tells us that South Africa has been given some as well.

It was responsible for motors catching on fire, carburettors melting and the destruction of many small motors. Now, this foul liquid we call petrol, only lasts for about three months, then deteriorates. Imagine what will happen on the 31st December 1999 when people store it in drums to power their generators when the Y2K problem cuts off the electricity supplies. It is clear that the schemers will also need to doctor up the diesel in a similar manner, to make life harder for the guinea-pigs.

Also, please note a further psychological ploy that was used by the petrol companies. They employed a woman to appear on television to calm our fears about this foul, dangerous, brew. Service station owners and male drivers were incensed, yet common decency required that you do not attack a woman as you might a man - the clever devils.

What About M.M.P. (Mixed Member Proportional)?

We used to have a normal political system called FPP (first past the post) and then **MMP** was suggested. 99% of New Zealanders didn't understand what it was all about so in it came. **It's new, so it must be good, was the thinking.**

Result? Chaos! A mass of small political parties working from time to time as coalition partners. Ex-Prime Minister David Lange, called it, *"A talking shop of madness."* The New Zealand 'Herald' reported an ex-Prime Minister of Australia also speaking vehemently against it.

'Herald', 6th March 1999 - *"MMP vote act of insanity - Hawke.*

"New Zealand's MMP system is a dog's breakfast", says former Australian Prime Minister, Bob Hawke.

The country had been in political heaven before it engaged in a collective act of national insanity by voting....for MMP, he told the Australia-New Zealand Chamber of Commerce in London yesterday.

Mr Hawke said, he always knew New Zealanders would live to regret their decision to go for MMP and would take the first opportunity to change it...." End quote.

A Funny Story

Politics has descended to a real low in the world's laboratory, New Zealand. This chapter is being written on the 24th March 1999. We had a series of Prime Ministers, all of whom, along with their at the time Minister of Finance, danced to the tune of the Adam Smith Institute philosophies, and the Mont Pelerin Society who have members both in the Business Round Table, and even within government circles.

Every thinking New Zealander agrees with Mr Lange and Mr Hawke that MMP is a national disaster. So also **did** our latest Prime Minister, Mrs Shipley.

'Daily Telegraph', 26th January 1999 - *"Prime Minister Jenny Shipley says she no longer believes First Past the Post (FPP) is the best electoral system for New Zealand.*
Mrs Shipley, an opponent of Mixed Member Parliament (MMP) when it was first introduced at the last election, said yesterday the real question now was whether New Zealanders had chosen the best form of proportional representation...." End quote.

A careful examination of the above report tells us the following:

1. She did not initially agree with MMP.
2. She dodges the issue of saying she likes it now by asking a hypothetical question as to whether or not we have chosen the best form. We may now ask the question, "What other form is there?"
3. It is important to notice the timing of her statement. It comes just after a visit to the Germans, who understand MMP, and then to Great Britain where Tony Blair has been primed by the Mont Pelerin Society to emulate N.Z. He will call his system Proportional Representation (PR) or similar. (In politics today, you must do as you're told.)
4. Of course she had to apparently change her tune. The alternative would certainly have been political suicide!

Chapter Seventeen
To Whet the Appetite

In the year 1999, the media told us about a strange phenom-enon taking place in the food industry. Genetic Modification (GM) trials were being conducted more vigorously by those involved in the food business. Two important items were being tampered with.

A)   Soy beans - the health professionals basic ingredient.
B)   Potatoes were having frog's genes and silk worm's genes injected into the DNA. The potato of course is the staple diet of many in the poorer nations.

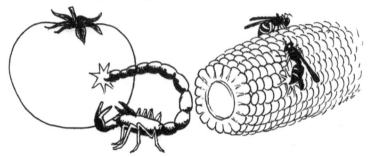

Q.   What person in their right mind would consider such a thing? Imagine the audacity of such money hungry manipulators, that they are prepared to fly in the face of obvious public opinion and fiddle with our food in this manner. Then to make matters worse, some in positions of authority, who know better, make speeches telling us that they are willing to eat these untested and unproven products.

At this point in history, money-hungry persons have now voted themselves the rights to inject foreign objects into our food chain. They need to be publicly identified, unmercifully thrashed and hung! How dare they continue to poison our means of staying alive?

When I wrote my book 'Second Warning' in 1984, I entitled one chapter "Seeds of Disorder" (page 51). This chapter explained stage 1 of the plan by these World Government controllers.

PBR - Plant Breeders Rights or PVR - Plant Variety Rights, where plant breeders have the authority to emasculate the seeds and turn them into a highly profitable, marketable product in the form of a hybrid. This provides for only one good season of growth. (See our book "Second Warning" 1984, pg49.)

It's only a theory I hold is it?

Chapter Eighteen
The Illuminati

Now, although this chapter may appear to be a little heavy for the average person, don't give up!

Firstly, the meaning. **Illuminati** - Those human beings initiated into the mysteries of the universe. The all-knowing ones who have the secret **gnosis** or the knowledge which gives them the right to rule over we lesser mortals.

Q.   Was there ever such a society in reality?

A.   'Encyclopaedia Britannica', Volume 12, 1963 - On the 1st May 1776, **Adam Weishaupt**, a Jesuit priest inaugurated this society in Bavaria. According to the encyclopaedia, it was a *"short-lived movement of Republican free thought...."* Never forget that when you are dealing with major newspapers, periodicals, books of facts, t.v. media and radio media, almost all of their owners or managers have links to Freemasonry and global government Illuminati-style groups e.g:

1.   Council on Foreign Relations (CFR)
2.   The Bilderbergers
3.   The Tri-lateral Commission
4.   The Club of Rome
5.   The Bank for International Settlements (BIS)
6.   The World Bank
7.   The G8 - It used to be called the G7 then they invited Russia to join. I'll bet they now regret that move!
8.   The International Monetary Fund (IMF)
9.   Adam Smith Institute
10.   Mont Pelerin Society
11.   Round Table groups
12.   Or, in the main, George Bush's **1000 Points of Light** referred to in his pre-Gulf war speech in 1990.

Remember, it was not short-lived. It still remains even to this day.

This man Weishaupt was obviously Satan's man for the job as he would infiltrate and change Masonry forever.[1] This obscure Jesuit-trained professor of canon law at the University of Ingolstadt in Bavaria, founded his society on the 1st May as this was a high witchcraft day.

The society was founded on a mixture of:

a.   Masonic secrets
b.   Islamic mysticism
c.   Jesuit mental discipline

An Illuminatus is a Master Mason who has received the **"light"** Masonry can bestow...[2]

Whatever these people are called, they form an elite cadre of "super-masons" with understanding of the craft **far beyond even the typical 33rd degree Mason.**

Is the Illuminati Still Around Today?

Yes, and they meet regularly in a hotel at a beautiful area of Switzerland called **Davos**. (Watch the international news for references to this small town.)

The Associated Press reported on the 29th January 1997 - *"World's elite meet in Geneva to wheel, deal and have fun.*

*Many of the world's power brokers and power seekers will wind their way up a narrow, avalanche-prone, Alpine valley in the remote eastern resort of **Davos** (Switzerland) this week for six days of deal-making, deep-thinking and fun.*

*Headliners at this year's World Economic Forum, which opens tomorrow, include **Microsoft billionaire, Bill Gates**, U.S. House Speaker, Newt Gingrich, top Russians and - as usual - key players from the Middle East.*

***The group of Illuminati**, including top scientists and*

experts in a range of fields, will have their pick of a bewildering array of meetings, discussions and dinners, many of them held simultaneously." (Author's note - This article lists Bill Gates amongst the Illuminati. How interesting that he should be included.)

"For some of the guests, however, the confabs are just an excuse to come. "If you look at the subjects of most of the debates, you can't imagine most people sitting through them,"said British Author, Bryan Appleyard.

Many of the government and corporate bigwigs will spend their time outside the Congress Centre in one on one meetings, cultivating potential partners in a deal or future contacts.

*Israeli Prime Minister, Benjamin Netanyahu, for example, has blocked out hours of time for sessions with other participants, including **Gates** and British Foreign Secretary, Malcolm Rifkind.*
***In fact, the Davos Forum, which began in 1971, has achieved its biggest fame as a backdrop for high stakes - political negotiations.** Netanyahu's predecessor, Shimon Perez, negotiated through the night in a hotel room with Palestinian leader, Yasser Arafat, in 1994, achieving breakthroughs in their peace efforts.*
The Prime Minsters of Greece and Turkey met in 1988 to smooth relations.
In 1990, soon after the Berlin wall came down, West German Chancellor, Helmut Kohl, sat with East German leaders, Hans Modrow, to move toward reuinification.
Sometimes differences are bridged within the Forum itself. In 1992, the then South African President, F.W. de Klerk, shared a platform with African National Congress leader, Nelson Mandela, and his Inkatha rival, Chief Mangosothu Buthelezi." End quote.

If Weishaupt wished to alter man's life in a manner only his supporters wanted, then it becomes imperative that ***"his goals be kept secret from his intended victims."***

He wrote, "The great strength of our order lies in its **concealment**, let it never appear in any place in its own name, but

always covered by another name and another occupation.[3]
Please note that **George Bush**, the man who introduced the NWO
belongs to the top secret Skull and Bones club. His secret name is
Poppy.

      Does this statement make sense to you? It certainly does to
me. Any hunter or fisherman will tell you that in order to catch
game, **"deception is the key word."**

Q.   Is there a difference between the Illuminati and
       Freemasonry?
A.   Initially, there was no connection but today, it is a different
matter. Freemasonry started well as a society of stone masons and
other artisans. According to the Encyclopaedia Britannica, Volume
12, 1963, in the year **1778** a friend of Weishaupt, **Baron Von
Knigge, infiltrated masonry in the upper degrees and often
managed to gain a commanding position**. Therefore it is only a
matter of degree. A high masonic degree corresponds to a position
in the Illuminati. A low masonic degree corresponds to a position
in the Masonic Lodge.

Q.   They say it is not a religion - Is it?
A.   Weishaupt even admitted he was forming a new religion. He wrote, **"I never thought that I should become the founder of a new religion."**[4]

Important Important Important

So the goal of the new religion became the substitution of the **"religious man"** with the **"illuminated man".** Man solving man's problems through the use of his mind.

Gnosticism is presumed to show the superior intellect of these satanically illumined world government planners. Their text book is the Kaballah. *"The gnostic mystery is based upon the hypothesis of emanations as being the logical connection between the irreconcilable opposite Absolute Spirit and Absolute Substance, which the Gnostics believe to have been co-existent in eternity."*[5] Hence, of course, the symbolic checkered floor in every Masonic Lodge.

The Goals of the Illuminati Conspirators

1.   The abolition of monarchy and all ordered government
2.   The abolition of private property
3.   The abolition of inheritance
4.   The abolition of patriotism
5.   The abolition of the family (i.e. of marriage and all morality)
6.   Abolition of all religion
7.   The introduction of the institution for the communal education of children

A Key Thought

In 1777, the year after founding his conspiratorial Illuminati group, Weishaupt was initiated into the masonic order - The Lodge Theodore of Good Counsel, in Munich, Germany.[6] His purpose in joining was not to become part of this benevolent order, but to **infiltrate it and then to control it altogether.**

Much of what is written about the Illuminati today comes from a book written in 1798 by Professor John Robison, a professor of Natural Philosophy at Edinburgh University in Scotland.

He entitled his book **"Proofs of a Conspiracy Against all the Religions and Governments of Europe, Carried on in the Secret Meetings of the Freemasons, Illuminati and Reading Societies."**

Author's note - With a title that long it is little wonder that the book did not become an instant best seller.

Professor Robison, himself a Mason, had been asked to join the Illuminati but he felt he should investigate the order before he joined. Robison concluded that the association had been formed **"for the express purpose of rooting out all religious establishments and overturning the existing governments of Europe."**

Audacious

Why do "educated" people chuckle knowingly, when investigators of the conspiracy mention the Illuminati. It has always been this way. Although the plan is outrageously clear, we note the following.

"The fact that the rulers of Europe wouldn't believe the goals of the Illuminati is a problem which is recurring all over the world today. It is difficult for the observer to believe that such a giant, well organised, conspiracy does exist, and that the goals they envisage for the world are real.
A Frenchman named Danton said this in French.
"Audacity, audacity, always audacity."[7]   End quote.

It was for this reason that the naughty boys at school found that they could get away with more mischief by sitting right under the teacher's nose in the front row rather than the back row of the class. I speak authoritatively as an ex-school teacher of 15 years experience.

Illuminati Concepts

If you are wondering whether the Illuminati conspirators have any regard for humanity, for goodness and integrity, now read this. *"Any activity, either moral or immoral becomes acceptable to the member of the Illuminati, as long as that activity promotes the goals of the organisation."*[8] End quote.

This will explain to the reader the secret power that guided the farcical impeachment process of President Clinton during the early part of 1999. The outcome was clearly decided before it all started. Clinton, full of self-confidence, went about his duties like a man possessed. He was told he was the chosen one. He would not lose his job. Ignore the impeachment, ignore his crimes, keep travelling, making speeches and bombing. Continue to emphasize two points:

a.   The American public are tired of all this trouble and want it over with;

b.   Let us get on with the business of running America.

       Strangely enough, a lot of people fell for this psychological deception!

       Three other Illuminati groups are also worthy of mention.

1.   The Bilderbergers in Europe
2.   The Tri-lateral Commission (T.C.)
3.   The Council on Foreign Relations (CFR)

       "The following is a list of the last nine presidents of the USA along with their past or present organisational affiliations:

a.   Franklin D. Roosevelt - Masonic Lodge
b.   Harry S. Truman - Masonic Lodge
c.   John F. Kennedy - CFR
d.   Lyndon B. Johnson - Masonic Lodge
e.   Richard M. Nixon - CFR
f.   Gerald R. Ford Jnr - Masonic Lodge/CFR

g.   *James E. Carter Jnr - CFR/TC*
h.   *Ronald W. Reagan - Masonic Lodge (Honorary)*
i.   *George H.W. Bush - SB/CFR/TC"*[9] End quote.

N.B. -

C.F.R. - Council on Foreign Relations
S.B. - Skull and Bones
T.C. - Trilateral Commission

---

[1]"Masonry - Beyond the Light" by Schnobelon, page 183
[2]"Masonry - Beyond the Light" by Schnobelon - page 184
[3]"The Unseen Hand" by Ralph Epperson - pages 81 & 82
[4]"The Unseen Hand" by Ralph Epperson - pages 81-84
[5]"The Secret Teachings of All Ages" by Manly Hall, pxxv
[6]"The Unseen Hand" by Ralph Epperson - page 82
[7]"The Unseen Hand" by Ralph Epperson - page 81
[8]"The Unseen Hand" by Ralph Epperson - page 81
[9]"En Route to Global Occupation" by Gary Kah - page 54

Chapter Nineteen
America's Role in the New World Order

"Not only were many founders of the United States Govern-
ment Masons, but they received aid from a secret and august body
*existing in Europe, which helped them to establish this country **for***
***a peculiar and particular purpose** known only to the initiated few.*

The Great Seal is the signature of this exalted body -
unseen and for the most part unknown - and the unfinished pyramid
upon its reverse side is a trestle-board, setting forth symbolically
the task to the accomplishment of which the United States' govern-
ment was dedicated from the day of its inception."[1]

As we write this chapter in late 1999, the peculiar and
particular purpose is now very clear. **The U.S.A. was designed for
the purpose of leading the rest of the world into enslavement,
under a one world government.**

There is now no longer any doubt about this!

Date - Friday, 20th June 1997. NBC News - **David Blume
filling in for Tom Brokaw; speaking to the President of the
U.S.A., Bill Clinton**.

Tape - 19.6.97 - *"David Blume with the president tonight.*
Thanks. Denver is an especially fitting site for this meeting of
world leaders and for the Russians to be in town. Over the years,
***from the Cold War to the New World Order**, the city's economy*
has found a way to thrive on world events."[2] End quote.

How is it that this term, New World Order, has been ban-
died around since George Bush's Gulf War speech but **it has never
been publicly defined by any politician?** Strangely enough, the
powers that be, do not want you to know its true meaning until they
have passed the point of no return.

Davos

The coach containing our tour group from New Zealand,
Australia and the South Pacific, wound its way up the long valley,
nestled amongst the snow-covered mountains of the Swiss Alps. A

feeling of excitement came upon us as we viewed this beautiful hotel, our accommodation, just up the road from the coach parking area.

After a top class meal that night, which included seconds of everything (unknown in many such establishments), we left the dining room to view the scenery. Walking up the hallway, **I found my attention rivetted on a large picture of Yasser Arafat**. It was at that very moment, the penny dropped. We were there, right in the very hotel where the secret one world government planners hold their secretive gatherings.

Davos - *"It's been called the "graduate school of the elite" and it takes place always at the same city in Switzerland. Davos, a very beautiful place. You can only get there if you're a grandee of international finance, if you're the head of an international corporation doing more than a billion dollars a year globally, you pay $28,000 a year to go, or you're a key figure in a Western agency or government that's important to the topics under discussion. So, to cut a long story short, one of the wire services....announced that this meeting was taking place... and said, "at the annual meeting of the* **Illuminati**.*"*[3] End quote.

"Is this all true?" I hear you cry.

We have shown you the actual text for you to study with your own eyes. If, after that reading, you still have a problem, it lies not with this author but with the Associated Press whom as you have already noticed, confirm the Illuminati's existence in this our day.

So there we have it, in black and white. We have been told by the "experts"on world matters that the Illuminati was a figment of conspiracy theorists' imaginations but this information tells us otherwise.

Points to Note

China is the wild card in the pack and along with Russia, will continue with their arrogant stance to be players in the New World Order game.

Divide Up the World

The Illuminati front groups like the **Bilderbergers** and the **Trilateral Commission** plan to divide the world up into 3 governmental zones with the aim of better control.

A)   The Asian Union
B)   The European Union
C)   The American Union (Davos, Switzerland)

Each one of these groups will have an enforcement army. Now you understand the title **"Trilateral Commission"**.

An interesting word of prophecy written about 96A.D. seems applicable at this point.

"And the great city was divided into three parts, and the cities of the nations fell, and Babylon came in remembrance before God, to give unto her the wine of the fierceness of His wrath."[4]

78

This giant city refers to the prophetic areas known as Mystery Babylon, the seat of power at this strange time of world history. As we move into the year 2000, watch all these events take place with lightning speed.

[1] 'The Secret Teachings of All Ages' by Manly Hall, pxc and xci
[2] 'Quinn in the Morning Show' - web site
[3] 'Quinn interview on the New World Order'.
[4] Revelation 16:19

Chapter Twenty
The Illuminati and America or America the Horrible

The song is called "America the Beautiful". No doubt it is still a naturally beautiful country, but because of some evil behind the scenes manipulation, it is no longer the land of the free, and the home of the brave.

You have already, I presume, read the chapter on the two founding groups in America. Remember the: Pilgrims' aim - religious freedom; Freemasons and occultists' aim - a peculiar and particular purpose i.e. to place Lucifer/Satan on the throne of the world.

A True Story

A dear friend of mine who lives in Johannesburg, South Africa, told me about a friend of his who used to study our books and tapes and agreed that this New World Order plan was satanic to the core.

One weekend, however, he attended a course for business-men who wished to succeed. The speaker was a man who had studied all the then-known arts of brain-washing and he himself had discovered a further technique.

When this businessman arrived home after the two day conference, my friend was shocked to discover that his business acquaintance had done a 180 degree turnabout and now extolled the virtues of a one world system.

To those readers of a more spiritual frame of mind, let me share with you about the power of black magic. Please do not be surprised, because you see, **we are not dealing with a political, economic or religious problem here**. This is an outright luciferian, satanic, devilish attempt to take over both your lives and mine. Believe me, **black magic is involved.**

"True black magic is performed with the aid of a demonia-cal spirit who serves the sorcerer for the length of his earthly life,

with the understanding that, after death, the magician shall become the servant of his own demon. For this reason, a black magician will go to inconceivable ends to prolong his physical life, since there is nothing before him beyond the grave.

The most dangerous form of black magic is the scientific perversion of occult power for the gratification of personal desire.

...A man will barter his eternal soul for temporal power and down through the ages, a mysterious process has been evolved which actually enables him to make this exchange.

...Though the demonism of the Middle Ages seems to have disappeared, there is abundant evidence that in many forms of modern thought - especially the so-called "prosperity" psychology, "will-power building", metaphysics and systems of "high-pressure salesmanship", black magic has merely passed through a metamorphosis and although its name be changed, its nature remains the same..."[1] End quote.

Okay. So now we understand that in this particular study, we are dealing with demonic spirits. Members of the Rationalists Association should really set aside time to live with true believers in Christ and have an open mind, willing at all times to learn.

Have you ever observed a person levitating off the floor? People with their eyes changing to all the colours of the rainbow, or a person spitting old, rotten teeth, and having a new set grow immediately? Have you seen an 89% disabled person supported by 3 friends suddenly straighten up, completely healed? Have you ever had a devil dog rip its way through the wall of your house in front of startled spectators?

I have and until you can explain these strange phenomena, I suggest you think very carefully about what you reading here!

Our seven books all have relevant information on the founding of America and so, I will simply recap.
1.   The Illuminati Freemasons' peculiar and particular purpose for America has been to place Lucifer/Satan on the throne of the world.[2]

2.	The United States corrupt Banking System (started in 1913 and is an Illuminati conspiracy) - their first task was to control the currency of that country. The setting up of this system was absolutely outrageous. The Illuminati conspirators set up a central bank and had the cheek to call it, "**The Federal Reserve**".

"The Federal Reserve System is not Federal, it has no reserves and it is not a system at all, but rather, a criminal syndicate."[3] End quote.

*"They had to avoid the name Central Bank, so it was named the Federal Reserve....It would be owned by **private individuals** who would draw profit from ownership of shares and who would control the nation's issue of money. It would have at its command the nation's entire financial resources....*

The method the conspirators used to defraud the American people was to divide the Federal Reserve System into twelve districts so that the American people could not call the bank a "central bank". The fact that the twelve districts had one director, called the Federal Reserve Chairman, apparently was not to be considered relevant.

Congressman Charles Lindbergh, warned the American people that the Federal Reserve Act....established the most gigantic trust on earth.

*When the President signs this act, the **invisible government** by the money power....will be legitimized. **The new law will create inflation whenever the trust want inflation. From now on, depressions will be scientifically created...**"*[4] End quote.

*"Thomas Jefferson, the Illuminati tool, Freemason and conspirator, who received the hooded messenger from Bavaria with the Illuminati seals in a velvet bag, seemed to know what was going to happen to his country. "If the American people ever allow private banks to control the issue of their currency, first by inflation, thereby deflation, the banks....will deprive the people of all property until their children wake up homeless on the continent their fathers conquered. **The issuing power should be taken from the banks and restored to the people to whom it properly belongs.**"*[5]End quote.

Wake up, Americans! You have had a private bank running your country since 1913 and your presidents and governments have been stupid enough to allow this situation to continue. The 31st December, 1999, is near at hand however. The Millennium Bug has begun the countdown.

What next have they prepared for us?

A. "The "Fed" is a private organisation; since the member banks own all of the stocks on which they receive tax-free dividends, it must pay postage like any other private corporation...In fact, America's elected officials know that the system isn't federal...It is privately owned and operated.
B. The system, after its creation in 1913, was in a position to loan the federal government large sums of money.
C. Every effort has been made by the Fed to conceal its powers **but the truth is - the Fed has usurped the government**.
D. It controls everything in the USA and controls all foreign relations.
E. It makes or breaks governments at will.
F. On May 23rd 1933, Congressman McFadden brought impeachment charges against the Federal Reserve Board, accusing them of causing the stock market crash of 1929, along with other charges. On two occasions, assassins attempted to kill McFadden with gunfire; later he died, a few hours after attending a banquet. There was little doubt that he was poisoned..."
G. The Federal Reserve will never allow itself to be audited."[6]
End quote.

Now, I guess this section answers a great many questions. Check a piece of U.S. currency. They all now read, "Federal Reserve Note". This is illegal currency. They should read "United States' Note"and should be issued by the U.S. government!

Author's note - Although they are very difficult to obtain, I have one in my possession. A bank manager friend mentioned that he has searched through thousands of U.S. notes but they were all issued by the private Federal Reserve.

Washington D.C.'s Position Important

Because that country was settled by Freemasons, along with the Pilgrims, the Masons had the knowledge to fill in a swamp, and build Washington D.C. right there. This is the only place the city could have been built as some power revealed to them, that just as Greenwich had to be situated exactly where it is now on the banks of the Thames River in London, Washington D.C. needed to be where it is on the banks of the Potomac River as a harmonic communications system could only operate from that very position. (Please look on the Internet for further information on this subject. The author of books available on it is called Bruce Cathie of Auckland, New Zealand.)

Symbols in Streets

a.   The Masons had their symbols of the compass and square built into the streets of Washington D.C. along with the satanic 5 pointed star, or pentagram. (See our book, "Better Than Nostradamus", pages 68 and 70. These Illuminati symbols both zero in on the White House **so each U.S. president has to contend with occult witchcraft from two different directions**.

b.   The main buildings in Washington D.C. i.e. the Lincoln Memorial, the White House, the United States Capitol Building, and the Jefferson Memorial; if lines are drawn from building to building, the result is a casket positioned according to masonic specifications. The ancient Egyptian obelisk, standing as a representation of the male generative organ raised up in Masonry, stands right in the middle of this casket shape, and thus becomes a focal point. (See our book, "The Devil's Jigsaw", pages 124-125).

The Illuminati and the Two Witchcraft Seals

If the American public learned what we have discovered about the seals on their $1 bill, they would be outraged. They were

84

designed in Bavaria by Weishaupt's Illuminati conspirators, carried across the Atlantic to Virginia by a hooded messenger, and handed to Thomas Jefferson in his drawing room. The year was 1782.

Thus, on the American dollar since 1933, the eye of Lucifer (Satan) in the triangle, hovers above the incomplete Egyptian pyramid of Giza. The meaning is clear. The illuminated Masons aim is to place their god Lucifer, on the throne of the world.

1. Many millions of folk worldwide have been misled into believing that the eye in the triangle is the eye of Almighty God. **This is not correct.**
2. The five Latin words on the left hand seal reveal clearly the eye and his aims. "Annuit Coeptis"- announcing the birth of "Novus Ordo Seclorum"- **a secular, heathenistic, godless, new world order (government).**
3. If not yet fully convinced, ask yourself this question - **"Why would Almighty God be setting up a new godless world government over which he had no control?"**
4. The so-called eagle on the right hand side is known to illumined Masons as a **phoenix**, rising from the ashes of the Tower of Babel. (This is all fully explained in our fifth book, "Better Than Nostradamus", pages 15-31.)

The Regime of Murder

The murder of John F. Kennedy has now been revealed as a conspiratorial cover up. The fatal bullet did not come from Oswald, it was fired from the front as declared by the examining doctor years later. More Illuminati lies. (See our sixth book, "The Devil's Jigsaw", page 95.)

The murder of defenceless people at Waco, Texas, was conducted by agents of the U.S. government. The video film, "Waco, the Big Lie", shows clearly a tank being brought in to set fire to the C2 gas already pumped into the compound. During that raid, 4 of Clinton's former bodyguards were found dead. All died from nearly identical wounds to the left temple. Their names were Steve Willis, Roberts Williams, Conway LeBleau and Todd McKeehan. The official story was that the Branch Davidian sect set fire to their own compound. More Illuminati lies. (See our sixth book, "The Devil's Jigsaw", page 96).

The secular media are now reporting that the U.S. government agents were responsible for burning these U.S. citizens to death. (Late 1999).

The Oklahoma bombing was conducted by persons unknown, along with the truck bombers. When an army man, a brigadier-general and demolition expert asked that the building not be demolished until he inspected it, the building was quickly ordered to be brought down. Why? Hitler conducted a similar operation in his day so the blame could be placed on the Jews. Is it possible that a branch of the U.S. government was somehow involved so that suspicion could be placed on the rapidly growing Militia movement?
Conclusion - A lying, cover up, with the Illuminati no doubt involved. (See our sixth book, "The Devil's Jigsaw" - page 96.)

Now, here is an interesting number....666. It is found initially in a prophecy dated 96 A.D. and it applies to the days leading up to the new millennium.

"Here is wisdom. Let him that hath understanding count the number of the beast: for it is the number of a man; and his number is six hundred, threescore and six."[7] End quote.

The U.S. Government Has 666 Seats

1	President
14	Cabinet Members

100	Senators
435	Representatives
9	Supreme Court Justices
13	Appeals Court Justices
90	District Court Chief Justices
4	Territory Justices

666

I ask you. Is a pattern beginning to emerge?

America is the World's Only Republic Run by Freemasons

The problem now becomes obvious. As the god of Freemasonry is Lucifer, and the founders aim was to place him on the throne of the world by the new Millennium, 1st January, 2001, the disintegration of that country has moved into top gear.

U.S.A. Your time is short!

---

[1]"The Secret Teachings of All Ages" by Manly Hall - PCI
[2]"The Secret Teachings" by Manly Hall - PXC and XCI
[3]"The Secrets of the Federal Reserve" by Eustace Mullins
[4]"The Unseen Hand" by Ralph Epperson - pages 171 and 173
[5]"The Unseen Hand" by Ralph Epperson
[6]*"The Unseen Hand" by Ralph Epperson - pages 182 and 183*
[7]Revelation 13:18

Chapter Twenty-One
The Illuminati Chooses U.S. Presidents

New Zealand 'Herald', 5th November 1980 - *"Websters in early for last word.*

The Republican challenger, Mr Ronald Reagan, has caused a major upset in the United States Presidential elections by beating Mr Jimmy Carter.

So, in effect, says the latest edition of Webster's dictionary, even though Americans do not go to the polls until later today to decide their President for the next four years.

Mr Reagan has been listed in the dictionary as the 40th President of the United States, along with his 39 predecessors...

*...The presumption or genuine mistake by the Chicago publishers, Consolidated Book Publishers, has dumb-founded the American Consul-General in Auckland... "**Unbelievable**", was his first word.*

...Auckland representatives of the publishers were just as surprised, and had no explanation...." End quote.

Another interesting fact to note is that there was an old Indian curse placed upon every U.S. President elected in a year divisible by 20. They were all to die in office and die they did.

We believe that the only reason President Reagan survived John Hinkley's shot was that a group of born-again businessmen had prayed for him and broken the curse in the Name of the Lord Jesus Christ. Abraham Lincoln was a non-mason and therefore thought he was able to design his own policies without fear of the Illuminati's influence. It cost him his life. John F. Kennedy tried to run the country his way without heeding Illuminati suggestions. It cost him his life. Richard Nixon also tried to buck the Illuminati system. It cost him his job. Ronald Reagan, it is now public knowledge, left the hostages in Iran until it became politically expedient to bring them home. Thus, those poor people suffered under horrific circumstances just so that Ronald would have some extra ammunition to prop him up in his re-election bid. Because he was a likeable old duffer, the Illuminati manipulated and used him to the max.

Even George Bush was affected by the power behind the satanic Illuminati during his tenure as U.S. president.

Christchurch 'Press', 2nd February 1993 - *"**George Bush** "knew about deal"*.

Former United States President George Bush, misrepresented his role and knowledge of the arms-for-hostages deal with Iran in 1985 and 1986 according to memoirs by former Secretary of State George Shultz.

In excerpts published by the 'Time' magazine, Mr Shultz said Mr Bush was at several meetings where the deal was discussed and went along with those following the scheme...

Mr Shultz wrote that as Mr Reagan's vice-president, Mr Bush "was in one key meeting, that I know of, on January 7, 1986, and he made no objection to the proposal for arms sales to Iran, with the clear objective (of) sic getting hostages released in the process.

*...**he saw Mr Bush on television saying it is inconceivable even to consider selling arms to Iran for hostages...**"* End quote.

This final statement attributed to our friend George, was nothing more or less than unmitigated lies.

The New World Order

Mikhail Gorbachev talked about it;
The news media talk about it;
The New Age movement talks about it;
The Freemasons talk about it;
Hitler mentioned it during World War II;
It is printed on the reverse side of the U.S. $1 bill;
It is the motto of Yale University;
but most important, George Bush, as President of the United States, announced it during his pre-Gulf War speech!
Stated simply, it means the New World Order will replace the Old World Order, we believe, after the Y2K (Millennium Bug)

crisis on midnight 31st December 1999. **It will culminate in each country which has privatised and has sold out their independence and sovereignty, becoming part of a Global Village.**

The word 'order', is a code word for a political, judicial, religious and economic system that will **turn the people of the world into slaves**. Each person, in order to buy or sell, will be forced to take a bio-chip in their forehead or right hand in order to buy or sell. If they refuse the mark, they will ultimately be killed.

Very soon a global leader will arise, nicknamed **the 'Beast'**, who will control the whole world system. Hitler was a Sunday School teacher when compared with this man of extreme evil! The New World Order is coming!

The Skull and Bones and the Illuminati

George Bush is a very important member of this society situated on the premises at Yale University. It is a German society, as was the Illuminati before it, and is also known by two other titles i.e. The Order and 322. Antony Sutton, in his book entitled "The Order", makes this statement. *"Above all, the Order is powerful, unbelievably powerful."* End quote.

Another point of interest is that the "initiated", i.e. the Patriarchs, only meet annually on Deer Island in the St Lawrence River. It was founded in America in 1833 and each year 15 new members are selected. About 500-600 of them are alive at any one time. George Bush was initiated in 1948.

An article written up in the 'Esquire' magazine tells us, *"One can hear strange cries and moans coming from the bowels of the tomb during initiation."*[1] End quote.

Four elements of the initiation ceremony are recorded:

a.   That the initiate has to lie naked in a coffin.

b.   That he is required to tell the secrets of his physical relations to fellow initiates.

c.   That Patriarchs dressed as skeletons and acting as wild-eyed lunatics howl and screech at new initiates.

d.   That initiates are required to wrestle naked in a mud pile.

Members of the Skull and Bones are required to leave the room if the name of their society comes up in conversation. The Illuminati of 1776, followed a similar strategy.

Skull and Bones is Pro-Nazi

This is an alien secret society which adds to its mysterious nature. Imagine a future U.S. President in the person of George Bush being a member of it!

A number of witnesses who have infiltrated this German secret society at Yale University tell of a literal Nazi shrine within its walls. One room on the second floor displays a number of swastikas. Other reliable witnesses have confirmed this story.

A Strange Phenomena

Scandalous information, I'm sure you will agree.

The question has been asked more than once. "Why do readers prefer the stories of **muck-rakers** to those of **political commentators**?

The answer is simple. The muck-rakers sell more papers. Within each person apparently, there seems to be a hidden desire for evil or even a sniff thereof. A little bit of scandal, shall we say. Wasn't it written somewhere, *"The heart is deceitful above all things, and desperately wicked: who can know it? I the Lord search the heart, I try the reins..."*[2]

Let us be gracious towards George Bush and also to all Masons and others caught up in this web of evil, mystery and intrigue even as Jesus, Himself, said, *"Father, forgive them; for they know not what they do."*[3]

George and Billy

'Challenge Weekly', 10th November 1998 - *"Evangelist Billy Graham returned to Tampa Bay, the birth-place of his world-wide ministry, where he received the call to preach and delivered his first street-corner sermons, more than 60 years ago, to share the gospel with a fourth generation.*

*...Graham preached with great strength each night, including a sermon on **"The Cross of Christ"**, the powerful symbol*

*of Christianity, as contrasted with **the emblem, a skull and crossed blades, prominently displayed** throughout the stadium.*

*...**Former President George Bush** appeared during the crusade to share his personal testimony of faith in Christ, and to speak of his admiration for Graham..."* End quote.

Thus we see both men made sure that the symbol of their very existence was on display.

I found this article very interesting, didn't you? Can you see the grace of God? No matter how far we become trapped in lies and deceit, there stands Jesus, still offering us **"grace"**.

Is it the Illuminati or the "illuminati"?

Many readers of the mainstream 'Washington Post', were probably shocked or puzzled by the following headline that appeared on page 23 of the 10th October 1998 edition: *"The Illuminati rally around the President."*

Was the 'Post' referring to the Illuminati, the capital 'I' version denoting the secret society of globalist elite who have been conspiring to seize and perpetuate control of the world for centuries, or the illuminati with a small 'i', the 'enlightened', if you can find a dictionary has even has the word in it.

...This brings to mind the use by the Associated Press (AP) a couple of years ago, of the little 'i' version of the word in describing a group of supposed 'world leaders' including House Speaker Newt Gingrich (R-Ga), in Europe to discuss global affairs, probably like those the Illuminati would no doubt be interested in.

In any case, it waxes strange that the mainstream media has suddenly decided to use a word that most dictionaries fail to mention, either the big "I" or small "i" versions. A coincidence perhaps...." End quote.

We don't think it's a coincidence, do we?

---

[1]"Esquire", September, 1977 by Ron Rosenbaum and "The Order" by Antony Sutton, p201
[2]Jeremiah 17:9-10
[3]Luke 23:34

Chapter Twenty-Two
Let's Be Fair

To this point, we have listed the havoc their so-called **reforms** have caused. However, not everybody agrees that the whole process was an utter failure. Please note the opening remarks of this speech given to the Institute of Economic Affairs (Fifth Annual Hayek Memorial Lecture), London, by Don Brash, Governor of the Reserve Bank of New Zealand. It is entitled, *"The Recovery of New Zealand.*

The revival of New Zealand's economy in the last few years follows one of the most remarkable economic liberalisations of all time...

...I myself was not involved in the earliest stages of the reform process, but became heavily involved in the taxation and monetary policy aspects of it at a fairly early stage. And like many of my peers, I had been brought up on an undiluted diet of **Keynesian economics** *and an almost undiluted diet of* **Fabian socialist politics***.*

...As well, **the first stage of the reform was carried out at high speed***....The case for fast and comprehensive, as opposed to gradual and piecemeal, action was cogently argued by Roger Douglas in a remarkable speech to a meeting of the* **Mont Pelerin Society** *in Christchurch in 1989.*

*...***"Opponents' fire is much less accurate if they have to shoot at a rapidly moving target."*** End quote.

Advantages of the Reforms

1. Working days lost through strikes have benefited employers.
2. The government of New Zealand is now collecting more revenue as it has sacked thousands of workers and cut back on funding for essential services i.e. education - health - police - fire service, etc.
3. In 1999, following the directions of the think tanks yet once more, they began gradually phasing out welfare, starting with single mothers under the age of 20. Imagine all the money they will save as nearly a quarter of New Zealanders

receive a state-funded pension or a benefit.

4.   Much of the State-owned enterprise assets have been sold overseas which saves our government members the worry of looking after them. Thus, they received a one of payment for something that was previously earning them billions of dollars i.e. Telecom-Railways-Banking Systems....

Any Cynic Can See This

Anyone who studies philosophy can at once see the advantages of being controlled from overseas. After all, who wants to run their own life? It is far preferable being controlled from the cradle to the grave. **Ask anybody who has lived under communism about the happy, contented life they led**. The New World Order that these people are building is therefore based on a philosophy that has never ever worked in the past and is a synthesis of:

Capitalism (thesis)

Communism (antithesis)

This, in brief, is the basic philosophy of the German philosopher Hegel, upon whose ideas the New World Order or one world government is being built.

To Sum Up

You thought that your elected government was running the affairs of your country, didn't you?

They used to, but no longer!

'New Citizen', July/August, 1996, page 6 - *"**Privatisation: Looting and Stealing** by the Money Power*.
The goal of the Mont Pelerin Society is to eliminate the nation state; on their way there, Mont Pelerin and its friends cheat and steal from the public like mad, through "privatisation". The process is quite simple.

*First, Mont Pelerin sets up a series of think tanks in the targeted country. Those think tanks are funded by local banks, stock-broking firms and other corporations which stand to make a fortune from "economic rationalism". These same banks and corporations sponsor politicians who are **greedy enough or stupid enough** to be brainwashed by Mont Pelerin doctrines.*

*   ***Once in government, these politicians make dirty, under-the-table deals to sell off precious state assets at a fraction of their true value to private financiers...."*** Break quote.

Cronyism

Continue quote - *"As the Mont Pelerin's main front organisation in New Zealand, the Business Round Table's individual and corporate members were the overwhelming beneficiaries of the destruction of the economy...*

Firms associated with the Business Round Table ended up with $12.542 billion of the $15.233 billion in privatised former state assets.

*...Mont Pelerin Society member ......, the **close friend and tutor** of Roger Douglas in economics, cashed in handsomely on "Rogernomics" over the 12 years of "reform" he and the Mont Pelerin Society have imposed on New Zealand.*

..... personal wealth has soared from $46 million in 1986 to $200 million today, making him the 4th richest person in New Zealand." End quote.

Let us however give him the benefit of the doubt. He may have won this money at the races.

Chapter Twenty-Three
They've Sold the Gold

Australia Sells Gold

"How can this be?" I hear you cry.

The "diggers" were outraged. You know those Aussie soldiers with the brims of their hats turned up. The term 'digger' was adopted as a symbolic gesture, showing the relationship between the early settlers who came to Australia to dig for gold, and the rugged masculine types who later on shouldered a rifle and went off to far away countries to fight for home, freedom and democracy.

'Herald Sun', Australia, 28th July 1999 - *"A wave of mine cut backs and closures has begun in Australia's goldmining industry as the price slump in the fabled metal deepens...There can be little doubt, the Australian mining industry is in crisis."* End quote.

'The Spectator', 22nd August 1998 - *"Gold is no longer an investment, but simply a commodity. There is no reason to own it, except as jewellery. The world financial system has changed, and gold has become obsolete within it. At around $285 an ounce, its price is close to its lowest level for 18 years and has nowhere to go but down. Anyone who owns any should rush to sell it now...its 2,800 year life as a currency is over..."* End quote.

Britain Sells Gold

'New Zealand Herald', 6th July 1999 - *"Plans by the British Government to auction 415 million tonnes of the nation's gold reserves is to face a double challenge from legal action being brought by a jeweller and lobbying from the World Gold Council.*
...The jeweller says, "It just doesn't make good business sense to sell gold at the lowest prices for 25 years and invest 40 per cent of the profits into an unstable Euro. I believe the Government has handled this in a reckless and irresponsible manner." End quote.

IMF Sells Gold

'Herald Sun', Australia, 14th June 1999 - *"Finance ministers from the world's seven richest nations have agreed on a debt relief plan for poor countries to be partly financed by selling gold held by the International Monetary Fund.*

The new proposals would boost a three year old debt relief program designed to help 40 of the world's poorest countries...

*Some ministers stressed that debt relief would be **conditional on economic reforms** by the countries that benefited from it..."* End quote.

The Cunning Old I.M.F. Spider

They are at it again. Readers of our previous six books will understand what is meant by the above heading. The world government promoters, using the IMF as their softening up tool, follow thee main planks.

1.   Loan money to individual countries
2.   Force them to sign the conditions
3.   The implementation of these conditions results in the loss of sovereignty and independence of each country.

Now, it becomes obvious that the IMF are so committed to this devious plan that they will go to extraordinary lengths to fulfill it, even to the point of selling up their gold reserves.

The Swiss Sell Gold

Hello, what's this we read? The Swiss franc has for centuries been tied to gold, and now we see that this last bastion of financial security is under siege. In a passage taken from an article entitled *"Goodbye Sovereign Switzerland"*, by Jane H. Ingraham, (http:www.thenewamerican.com/tna/1999/07-19-99/vo15 no15 swiss.html.) we quote in part.

"Without a murmur of dissent, the seemingly impossible was accomplished. Lacking understanding, the Swiss people voted this spring to end the unique soundness of their currency as well as

*their country's financial power and independence. Oblivious to the consequences of abandoning the Swiss franc's tie to gold, the people of Switzerland - the world's only direct democracy - approved a new constitution that abolishes the traditional gold convertibility that for generations made the Swiss franc literally **"as good as gold"**.*

*...In 1933, FDR stripped Americans of their gold under false pretences....As a matter of necessity, the Swiss franc's disciplinary tie to gold had to be abolished...the Swiss people would have to be made to do it to themselves...**using the suffering of the Jewish people as a bait.***

*...The charge: Swiss banks still held gold deposited by Jews who became victims of theHolocaust...Overlooked was the fact that in the 1950's, and again in 1962, Swiss banks formally investigated the dormant accounts of persons who may have died in the war, and paid out tens of millions to survivors and Jewish causes. In spite of this, the pressure was so intense that the Swiss government was forced to agree to convene an Independent Commission of Eminent Persons to audit the bank's records yet again. The Commission's chairman was none other than **Paul Volker of Federal Reserve fame**...*" Break quote.

This action could very easily be labelled, **"Goat Guards the Cabbage Patch."**

Please note that under the New World Order plans, or global government plans, **"speed" is the key word**, otherwise people will wake up to the evil nature of the plan and try to stop it.

Continue quote - *"...In the past, Swiss citizens had always been allowed as much as a month to scrutinize and debate a single constitutional change; this time they had to decide **very quickly**, without debate, on more than 100 articles containing profound modifications to their mode of government, their military and their culture. Obviously, **haste** was necessary to prevent the Swiss from realising that their laws, rights and customs were being subsumed under international edicts and mandates, including a perfidious attack on the traditional family.*

99

*...**The term "Swiss Nation" has been replaced by "people"** **amounting to an abandonment of national identity.***

*...The nature of Switzerland's citizen-soldier army, unique in the world, will be wiped out. In spite of popular refusal and opposition in the past, **Switzerland's soldiers will now serve with UN troops, abandoning the traditional army neutrality.***

*...The extinction of the sovereignty of Switzerland, should come as a fearful warning to Americans. When George Bush repeatedly referred to the **New World Order** he was helping to bring about at the time of the Gulf War, he never bothered to provide the details..."* End quote.

And so, this gives us some insight into the devious minds of these world government planners, and the lengths to which they will go to execute their surreptitious plans.

Gold is Finished as a Currency

An analyst at the South African stock exchange puts it this way. **"Once you question its mystical value, you see it has no value at all. It's becoming a barbarous relic!"** End quote.

Do you realise that this very situation was predicted in the year 48 A.D.

Some years ago we were holding lectures in Penang, Malaysia. I made the statement that cash was going to be cancelled and that a new economic system would take its place. I saw a very well-to-do looking Asian woman lean across and whisper something to one of my friends. After the meeting had concluded, I asked my friend what she had said. He chuckled, "That was so funny. She was panic-stricken, being one of the wealthiest people in this city. She had just finished whispering to me *"I'll have to invest in gold"*, when you read the prophecy!"

*"Go to now ye rich men, weep and howl for your miseries that shall come upon you. Your riches are corrupted, and your garments are motheaten. **Your gold and silver is cankered,** and the rust of them shall be a witness against you, and shall eat your flesh*

100

as it were fire. Ye have heaped treasure together for the last days."[1] End quote.

To Asians, gold has always been an unassailable hedge against currency fluctuations. Sorry, it's all over!

---

[1]James 5: 1 - 2

Chapter Twenty-Four
The Y2K Bug

A highly organised problem created by the U.S. government. (See 'Time' magazine, 18th January 1999, for information re: 1957 and 1967.)

1957 - Designed by Grace Hopper and team of scientists.

1967 - Ratified by the U.S. National Bureau of Standards. Federal Information Standard #4 that contained the standards for the calendar date. A six digit code was specified to represent the year, month and day with only units and tens of the year to be recognised.

Gary North, an American campaigner for people to recognise the dangers of Y2K said, *"Everything stops if the power grid goes down. If the lights go out at the dawn of the 21st century, the failure will be permanent because the computers that control the grid will be un-fixable if there isn't enough power to run them. **The blackout will trigger the collapse of civilisation!**"*

In our book, 'Final Notice', published in 1989, on page 65, we have printed the first clues that a Y2K like crisis was going to be engineered. These plans have been in existence since the 1930's.

"We shall create....a universal economic crisis whereby we shall throw upon the streets whole mobs of workers simultaneously. These mobs will rush delightedly to shed the blood of those whom, in the simplicity of their ignorance, they have envied from their cradles and whose property they will then be able to loot.
Ours they will not touch because the moment of attack will be known to us, and we shall take measures to protect our own.
We shall create an intensified centralisation of government in order to grip in our hands, all the forces of the community.
If we give the nations of the world a breathing space, the moment we long for is hardly ever likely to arrive." (Author's

note - Remember, all reforms must be conducted at full speed.)

"In order that the masses themselves may not guess what they are about, we further distract them with amusements, games, pastimes and passions.

We at last definitely come into our kingdom by aid of coups detat prepared everywhere for one and the same day after the worthlessness of all existing forms of government has been definitely acknowledged....

We shall see everything without the aid of the official police."[1] End quote.

A forecast of Sergius Nilus - *"One can no longer doubt it. Satan with his power and his terrors, the Antichrist - is about to mount the throne of universal empire."*

We are here, my friend - we are here!

Doubt It Not

The New World Order, announced by Skull and Bones member, ex-U.S. President George Bush, commences at 12:01 a.m., 1st January 2000.

The little country of New Zealand, situated in the South Pacific, was chosen as the **laboratory** for the demonic plans borrowed from the Adam Smith Institute in London and rehashed by another think-tank called the Mont Pelerin Society in London.

These ridiculous policies were adopted by certain members of the Business Round Table and also certain government members who began to implement them in earnest in the year 1987.

During the month of October 1999, this author held lectures in both London City, and also County Armagh in Ireland. It was highly noticeable that the media on that side of the world refrained from warning the populace of the impending danger.

Can You Believe This?

A tiny cutting in the London 'Financial Times', October 1999, read thus - *"Blitz to ease bug fears.*

All 26 million households in Britain will receive an official millennium bug "anti-panic", handbook from the Government next month in the biggest campaign of its kind since the infamous AIDs pamphlet of the mid-eighties...

*The glossy 24 page booklet will go out in the **first and second weeks of November**, making it the bulkiest national Government door-drop in living memory.*

*The document is aimed at easing fears about the impact of the millennium computer bug and **reducing the chance of a mass panic reaction**.*

Ministers are concerned that fear of the bug could cause more problems than any computer problems..." End quote.

Q.   Why is this?
A.   Because "the City" in London is a crucial financial centre.

A Simple Analogy

The wall of the giant dam has developed cracks and already water is leaking through. A fat glossy booklet is hastily prepared, but not given out to the townsfolk in the valley below. The Mayor explains, "We don't want fear and panic from the townspeople, do we? We will give the information out just as the main structure is about to collapse."

However, notice the contrast 12,000 miles away in New Zealand and Australia where the papers are packed full of information regarding it.

'Melbourne Age', 5th October 1999 - *"Most of the world's top computer experts plan to stockpile food, water and cash before the Y2K bug bites. But they are putting everyone else off-guard, lulling people into a false sense of security with their complacency and slackness. Says who? The world's top computer experts, that's who!"* End quote.

A True Story

Whilst in London, in the month of October 1999, I phoned some friends who live in that country.

Self - "Hello, it's Barry speaking. I'm just ringing to find out your husband's whereabouts and to make enquiries as to any preparations you two have made for the millennium bug.

Friend - "Yes, Barry. Here's is my husband's current contact number and regarding the millennium bug, I was down at the doctor's surgery yesterday. His waiting room was packed with elderly people all receiving inoculations against it."

Okay - Here We Go!

Here is a further list of headlines safely stored away in my filing cabinet. It makes for a very strong case, you will finally agree?

➤ *Henry Kissinger will withdraw all his money before 2000.*
➤ *Michael Foot says 12 large Great Britain financial companies are behind in preparations.*
➤ *France - 30% of the computers will fail.*
➤ *In the state of Maine, U.S.A., 2000 cars and lorries have been classified as horseless carriages (October 1999).*
➤ *The Israeli electric power companies are not prepared.*
➤ *Hawaii's electric power companies are three years behind.*
➤ *The American Samoan Island of Tutuila has spent three years getting ready - power, water and sewage. They hold they are safe now.*
➤ *Japan is nowhere near ready. Hospital staff are being trained to use manual equipment.*
➤ *Rabbis in Israel have been asked for permission for strategic service personnel to be able to work on the Sabbath.*
➤ *196 countries are unsafe to travel to.*
➤ *Computer crooks pretending to fix the problems set it up for other evil purposes.*
➤ *Airlines in 34 countries are not ready.*

➤ *Don't travel to Ukraine or Russia, take cash to Egypt and Fiji.*

➤ *The Channel Tunnel will be closed on the changeover night.*

➤ *The biggest problem - how will the bug affect the world's f inancial system?*

➤ *A bunker has been set up in Canberra to advise the world of problems.*

➤ *The police can use force and government can take over businesses in Australia.*

➤ *U.S. and Russian missile sites are unsafe.*

➤ *Shops selling survival gear say people are shy and afraid of friends' comments.*

➤ *Bankers in the U.S. have spent $8 billion dollars on the problem. They do not like funny remarks by comedians and others.*

➤ *Transport agents in Malaysia are practising using candles and rubber stamps.*

➤ *The millennium bug will savage the Euro.*

➤ *London Investment companies are closing for three months.*

➤ *Suppliers will bring down large firms. Out of 6000 suppliers to Chrysler, 2000 are not ready.*

➤ *Fijian and other Pacific Islands' phone systems are a mess.*

➤ *The Dutch are apathetic about the Y2K problem. Holland will go down.*

➤ *Diplomats are being taken from non-prepared countries.*

➤ *Only one-fifth of Americans are preparing.*

➤ *Nuclear power plants take five months to cool down. They all should have been shut down in July 1999.*

➤ *In Russia, 74 nuclear powered submarines are in the cool-down stage.*

➤ *London - Army, police and fire service say, "No hope of controlling all the problems.*

➤ *45% of Y2K experts worldwide are worried.*

➤ *The Amish religious group in the U.S.A. are not worried by Y2K.*

➤ *Computer expert Ed Yourdon, says* **"Keep out of the cities."**

- *In Canada, Operation Abacus is the government plan. Ships will supply some power for cities.*
- *In the town of Dimona, Israel, 30,000 need to be evacuated from the nuclear power area.*
- *Not enough room on the ground if all the planes land. There must be **80%** of them in the air at all times.*
- *Britain warns, "Keep away from S.E. Asian airports."*
- *Central and South America, Asia and Africa are dangerous - not Y2K ready.*
- *C.I.A. warns of lack of heat. Massive winter problems for the northern hemisphere.*
- *Imbedded chips - massive problems with oil platforms.*
- *100 systems with 10,000 microchips.*
- *Farmers are to receive advisory kits regarding milking, irrigation and grain storage.*
- *U.N. troops are training on U.S. and Canadian soil - why?*
- *London hospitals warn that 600-1500 will die due to Y2K.*
- *2000 bug could kill 75 New Zealand patients. Beware of hospitals.*
- ***If power fails, everything else will fail and all efforts have been of no avail.***
- *Y2K is a world-wide crisis. Even if it is fixed, it will collapse again on the 29th February 2000 (a leap year).*
- *U.S. Government will declare a state of emergency. Suspend the Constitution. Invoke FEMA. Call on UN troops to arrest and imprison dissenters.*
- *Ready for a disaster. The Queensland Government will be able to declare a State of Disaster on New Year's Day next year if the millennium bug interrupts the supply of electricity, gas or water, following introduction of legislation yesterday.*
- *Welcome to the year 2000 and the New World Order.*

---

[1]"Protocols of the Learned Elders of Zion". A Masonic plan fraudulently attributed to the Jews.

Chapter Twenty-Five
Twin Problems Looming

On page 147 of our first book 'Warning', dated March 1978, we included a portion of a vision as seen by the late Daisy Osborne, entitled, *"I Saw the Face of the Earth Changing"*. As the wife of a respected missionary evangelist, T.L. Osborne, this woman's credibility is about to be vindicated, possibly even within the space of a few short months.

Remember that this vision was seen 21 years before this book went into print.

Coming Judgement

"In a vision, I saw the face of the earth changing. The shape of America was drastically altered and reduced in size through terrible disasters. Hunger and suffering were everywhere. The devastation caused by volcanic eruptions and fires was widespread and horrifying.

During this awful holocaust, I saw Christians clustering together from all walks of life and many church affiliations. They did not care whether they were Baptists, Lutherans, Mennonites or Pentecostals; the tie that bound them in that desperate hour was their common faith in Christ.

Sometimes in large families, a sudden death or tragedy will re-knit broken ties. And so it is in the Christian family; doctrinal prejudices have divided God's children - there's dissension, reprisal, jealousies, strife, offense. But after the terrifying cataclysm which the Lord allowed me to see, all of the evils of sectarianism and apostasy vanished amidst the Christian's desperate struggle to draw strength from one another.

Those who had been lukewarm cast aside besetting sins and sought identity with the true believers. I saw cigarettes being discarded, pills being tossed, social drinkers lamenting their indulgences, marital cheaters seeking to make amends. A new sense of values gripped the conscience of believers. The "new" morality standard and modern license for laxity was like a remorseful hangover.

Most of the Christians I saw in this visitation were amazed that we were experiencing the terrible day of the Lord, and witnessing His wrath and judgment. Many social Christians were ill-prepared. Their frivolous, unwatchful, imprudent lives had been gambled on mercy which they thought required no reckoning - ever. I saw them - hordes of them - lost among the rebellious and rejecters of Christ.

As I looked, I could see where mountains were flattened. Believers were fleeing to the desert to take shelter in caves and rocks and hills.

...All but a very few were full of remorse. Lamentations could be heard everywhere, such as:

"Had I known the end was so near, I could have done more to influence my family to
follow Christ."

"I never realised things were so urgent."

"I planned a life of full-time service - eventually, but I thought other matters were
more important now."

"If I could live this last year again, I'd be facing today differently."

"And to think, I've saved everything - only to lose it all."

"I thought someone would let me know about such a terrible happening as this.
Didn't anyone know?"

But it was heartening to observe that during the fearsome disaster, unshakeable faith held like an anchor among the true Christians. They knew that would soon see the Son of Man coming in the clouds of Heaven with power and great glory.

"And when these things begin to come to pass, then look up, and lift up your heads, for your redemption draweth nigh."[1]

The peace that I had experienced all through the vision was unearthly. Faith in the Lord Jesus Christ had stabilised the believers, there was peace even amidst catastrophe.

But the look of utter dismay and horror on the faces of unbelievers kept haunting me. Their cries of doom still rang in my ears.... " End quote.

Is the Y2K Problem Mentioned in the Prophecies?

See what you think!

About the year 520 B.C. a Jewish prophet called Haggai wrote, *"For thus saith the Lord of hosts; Yet once, it is a little while, and I will shake the heavens, and the earth, and the sea, and the dry land;*

And I will shake all nations, and the desire of all nations shall come: and I will fill this house with glory, saith the Lord of hosts."[2]

Explanation - Men would find it most difficult to set up a world-wide earthquake, hurricane or flood, but God can allow man to create his own judgment in the form of a catastrophic global computer collapse. But that is not all - there is more!

Although the main problem will commence on the 1st January 2000, in the little South Pacific country of New Zealand about 11 a.m., further information has reached our office which now makes sense of the references to the heavens and the earth and the sea, and the dry land all being shaken.

There is a second problem which will run concurrently with the Y2K bug.

New Zealand 'Herald', 24th March 1999 - *"Flareup in sunspot activity threat to satellites and electricity grid.*

Solar flare activity, predicted for early next year could fry communications satellites and send vast sheets of geomagnetic electricity through the earth, blowing transmitters and cutting power in some parts of the world.

...The half cycle of sunbursts builds to a height every 11 years and reaches a climax every 22 years.

...There is growing evidence that even satellites built to withstand the sun's activity, are at risk.

...For every three satellites over North America there is often one on standby. However, there are no standbys over Australia and New Zealand...sunspots increase relatively quickly and decay slowly. They affect the ionosphere and could cause blackouts..." End quote.

Then again, about 68 A.D., an unknown writer predicted a similar scenario. *"Whose (God's) voice then shook the earth: but now he hath promised, saying, Yet once more I shake not the earth only, but also heaven.*

*And this word, Yet once more, signifieth the removing of those things that are shaken, as of things that are made, **that those things which cannot be shaken may remain.**"*[3] End quote.

Explanation - "There is a plan and a purpose behind all of God's actions. Unlike man, He is not given to waffling and making obscure, meaningless statements.

Reasons for this Shaking

The purpose is to assist mankind to make sensible choices as to what really counts in life. It has become more than clear that as the New World Order plans proceed, everything that we have held dear is being surreptitiously stripped away. The wise amongst us are asking the following questions.

A.   Who am I?
B.   Where did I come from - what are my origins?
C.   What am I doing here - what is life's purpose?
D.   Where am I going - is the grave truly the end?
E.   What is happening to the secure and stable lifestyle that I once knew?
F.   What will stand me in good stead and give me security as my world-view is put under extreme pressure?
G.   When my life comes to an end, what will have been the purpose of my existence?
H.   When all else that I trusted in is shaken, what do I possess that will continue on beyond this life into the next?

Dad's Good Advice

I guess some sons have reason to despise the man they called "Dad". On the other hand, some loved and admired theirs'. What was your dad like - good or hopeless?

Brought up in a family of 11 children whose mother died while they were young, my Dad used to delight my two sisters and I by repeating the names of his siblings with the rapid staccato sound of a machine gun. I have this list on the wall of my office to this day - "Edgar - Ted - Jack - Bob - Alice - Alf - Bill - Gert - Else - George - Mill."

My Dad, Ted, was a very happy, laid back, committed Christian. He loved to joke yet his love for the Lord who saved Him was very strong. **He taught me the valuable lesson of balance. "Be yourself - be real. Don't become legal or lax in your Christianity but hold on to it firmly as the only reliable foundation in life."**

In the year 1962, he was speaking at a gathering of Christian believers at a N.Z. town called 'Taupo'. His final words were, **"Even if we are unfaithful, God remains faithful."** His heart stopped beating and he fell. Chairs flew in all directions and pages from his open Bible fluttered to the floor.

My Dad, the man I loved and admired, was with the Lord Jesus. Brought up in a rough atmosphere with no mother, yet he and his older sister Millie, chose the Lord's way. I'm so glad they did. *"Thank you, Dad."*

I well remember him teaching me the first Psalm from the Bible, showing clearly the end result of the two lifestyles. With God, we are like a tree planted by a river - strong and healthy. Without God, we have no roots and no foundation. We become withered and miserable. It may do some readers the world of good to visit an old-age pensioner's home and observe with your own eyes, these two groups clearly portrayed.

Read this slowly and think about it. Your future could depend on your perception of God's divine wisdom.

"Blessed is the man that walketh not in the counsel of the ungodly, nor standeth in the way of sinners, nor sitteth in the seat of the scornful.

But his delight is in the law of the Lord; and in His law doth he meditate day and night.

And he shall be like a tree planted by the rivers of water, that bringeth forth his fruit in his season; his leaf also shall not wither; and whatsoever he doeth shall prosper.

The ungodly are not so: but are like the chaff which the wind driveth away.

Therefore the ungodly shall not stand in the judgment, nor sinners in the congregation of the righteous.

For the Lord knoweth the way of the righteous: but the way of the ungodly shall perish."[4] End quote.

I've been with many dying people over the years. The contrast between the believer and the unbeliever becomes very clear and provides a stark contrast in times of crisis or bereavement. ***"One dieth in his full strength, being wholly at ease and quiet....And another dieth in the bitterness of his soul, and never eateth with pleasure."***[5]

To the reader of this book who was brought up in a godless home, I say, "Despite the information provided here, please don't skip the underlying message. We all need to get right with God."

A sign on a back road in Canada may prove to be relevant at this point. "Choose your rut carefully. You could be in it for some time."

---

[1]Luke 21:28
[2]Haggai 2:6-7
[3]Hebrews 12:26-27
[4]Psalm 1
[5]Job 21:23&25

Chapter Twenty-Six
What on Earth is Going On?

Halfway through the year 1998, we were on the island of Tutuila in American Samoa. A friend who was involved at leadership level in ASPA (American Samoa Power Authority), upon our request, took us along to view the power system that provided for the island's energy needs.

Once in the control room, it was made abundantly clear that we must stand in the middle of the room so as not to bump any of the finely tuned computers. Our friend Gary Sword, told us that it had taken them three solid years of work to get everything up and running to such a degree that they could guarantee power, water and sewerage for the island, come 1ˢᵗ January 2000.

The next day, to our surprise and horror, we learned that the State of Hawaii situated to our north, was three years behind in the upgrading of their electricity systems. We have friends on all these islands and are really concerned for them.

We have written a total of six books prior to this one and to explain everything again in full detail would be an impossible task. A precis of major facts is therefore in order. An understanding of Y2K will then make sense. We will include the book title with each piece of information.

Precis

1. For 200 years there has been a plan afoot to set up a one world government of a secular nature. Check any American one dollar bill past 1933 and on the reverse side, you will see the two witchcraft seals. ('Better Than Nostradamus'.)

2. Many secret and not so secret societies are involved in the detail and implementation of these plans. **George Bush in his 1990 pre-Gulf War speech, referred constantly to a**

New World Order, which is the coded phrase for a One World Government. Jimmy Carter before him called the plan "Global 2000" - the idea being that a set of surreptitious manipulations would be artificially created for each national government and then the answer to the created problem would be offered by those who created the problem in the first place. This clever piece of footwork comes out of the philosophies of a **German philosopher named Hegel.**

3. Ex-President George Bush, his father before him and his son, George Bush Jnr, all belonged to a German secret society during their days as students at Yale University. The names of this most powerful club are varied - **'The Order', 'The Skull and Bones', '322'.** It is strictly occultic and because it follows the Hegelian dialectic or the philosophies of the German Hegel, it is dedicated to the tricky task of a) creating a chaotic situation with each country's financial systems b) encouraging ethnic unrest and a desire for minority groups who originally lived peacefully with the majority group, to begin a vicious struggle for independence and self-rule. Hegel put this very succinctly when he said, *"For this system of Hegelian philosophy comes the historical dialectic i.e. that all historical events emerge from a **conflict** between opposing forces."*[1] Hegel divided these two groups into **'thesis'** and **'antithesis'**, the idea being that you let them battle it out; even killing is perfectly in order, then at a suitable point, the organisers of this demonic scheme say, "That's enough fighting now, boys!" The general populace are left dazed, confused, weary of war and longing for an answer. Who provides this answer? The secret controllers of this world's affairs, called by George Bush **'1000 points of light'**. Hegel's idea was to bring them to the negotiating table and organise a form of peace which he called **'synthesis'. Thus thesis plus antithesis equals synthesis.**

4. At this time of writing, one may read the daily newspaper or watch television and see the Hegelian dialectic in action, yet at different stages of development in each country, it is, simply put, demonic manipulation.

5. Thesis	Antithesis
U.S.A.	U.S.S.R.
South African ANC - Mandela	Zulus IFP - Buthalezi
Ireland - Unionists - North	Sinn Fein and the
	IRA - North and South
Yugoslavia - Serbs	Albanians
Africa - Hutus	Tutsis
U.S.A. - Whites	Native American Indians
Australia - Whites	Aborigines
Indonesia	Timorese
Sri Lanka	Tamil Tigers
Israel	Arab Nations
New Zealand - Whites	New Zealand Maori

Now, please notice that the U.S. A. and the old U.S.S.R. are in a synthesis mode. The ANC and the Zulus are also in a synthesis mode as are Northern and Southern Ireland. The other nations continue on with their supposed fight for freedom, independence and democracy, only to find that they were simply pawns being moved by subtle manipulators. Sadly, their blood is being shed for nought as they will soon discover. The bubble will burst at the end of 1999.

---

[1]"The Order"by Antony Sutton - page 119

Chapter Twenty-Seven
Come Back Henry Kissinger

Strangely enough, that was the giant headline we found in Great Britain's 'Sunday Telegraph', 13th June 1999. The following article which praises Kissinger's foreign policy exploits concludes in the following manner. *"....As always, Kissinger's prose is clear, declarative and epigrammatic."* In the margin, my personalised comment reads, **"What?"** Let us read some of the article however.

"When Dr Kissinger was National Security Advisor to President Nixon and Secretary of State to President Ford, no-one ever suspected him of incompetence. He was sometimes wrong and sometimes devious. He was often overbearing. And as this book reveals, (his third volume of memoirs), he was occasionally self-serving. But Kissinger was a brilliant diplomatist, both a profound theorist of foreign policy and a skilled practitioner.

He was at once a conceptual strategist and a deft tactician. With equal facility, he assessed the historic implications of events and at the same time, carefully plotted the next step in a negotiation...You end up with the strong impression that here was a man who knew what he was doing....

Moreover, says Kissinger in one of his recurring themes, the Unites States was pulling itself apart in a tumultuous debate about national purpose and America's role in the world..." Break quote. (The next section that you are about to read will show you why Kissinger's books are such that once you have put them down, you can't pick them up again.)

Continue quote - *"The country's "congenital oscillation between overextension and abdication" was exacerbated by a fundamental clash between a resuscitated Wilsonian liberalism, which evaluated foreign policy on the basis of moral imperatives, and the emergence of a neo-conservatism, which saw foreign policy as a relentless ideological crusade...."* End quote.

In the many biographies about this man, most writers point out that although his readers and listeners rarely understand what he is saying, his readers and listeners, captivated by a strange aura that accompanies him, **"wish to make his words their own"**.

I therefore encourage any reader who feels this way to make the quote printed above, "your own". The reason for this is that I feel that I can live without it!

Kissinger - The Public Relations Man for the New World Order

What do we know about him?

He is a student of European political history. He has studied the political lives of such 'great' men as Castlereagh (England), Bismark (Prussia), and Metternich (Austria). He uses their political cliches and phrases during his peace negotiations i.e. **the balance of power, a global concept**.

'Letters to the Editor' for 'Daily Mail', England, 6th July 1999 - *"What's surprising about Henry Kissinger is not the fact that he was awarded the Nobel Peace Prize, but how a former Austrian Jeep driver could become the most powerful man in the U.S., that bastion of democracy, without ever receiving a single vote.*

He was never a representative, nor a congressman, nor a senator, nor a governor, yet when Nixon was mentally stressed, he was the most powerful man in the world. How he came to be there is a mystery..." End quote.

He is also very popular amongst his own Israeli people.

'Jerusalem Post', 23rd November 1998 - *"Ben Gurion University of the Negev, has announced that it has bestowed an honorary doctorate yesterday on former U.S. Secretary of State, Henry Kissinger, in New York, for his extensive efforts to achieve peace and reconciliation among nations. The citation noted that the Nobel Peace Prize winner **"never wavered in his staunch support of the Jewish people and the State of Israel"**.* End quote.

Please note that this latter phrase is highly important as the prophets make it abundantly clear that a non-religious Jew will confirm a peace treaty between the Jews and the Arabs for a period of seven years and then break it again after only three and a half years. Here is part of a transcript as written by Jeremy Paxman, Belfast.

'Letters to the Editor', 'Daily Telegraph', England - *"....I asked Dr Kissinger whether he felt a "fraud" on receiving the Nobel prize for 'bringing peace' to Vietnam because the peace accords did not do so..."* End quote.

Christchurch 'Press', 9th July 1994 - *"A winner of the Nobel Peace Prize who has also been described as a serial murderer, Henry Kissinger, in the 1970's was one of the most powerful people on earth."* End quote.

We quote herewith, snatches from the book *"Diplomacy"*. *"Apart from his humour, Kissinger was famed for his temper. He has said of his father, a Jewish refugee from Nazi Germany, that he was far too disciplined to inflict his emotions on others, and "disciplined" remains one of Kissinger's favourite words of praise....*
*"Because my general approach to negotiations was to **try and discover the end point at the very beginning**...*
...the book can also be viewed as an unending chess game, in the sense that history has no end." End quote.

The Melbourne 'Age', 27th March 1999 - *"A media headline, A Flatterer's Memoir gives us further insight into this man and his methods...*
"There can't be a crisis next week", Kissinger joked in 1970. "My schedule is already full."...
These days where there is a crisis, Kissinger doesn't have to deal with it, just comment on it. The media want to know his reaction to everything.
*...It is 23 years since Kissinger left high office, yet **he still has an aura of power**.*

*...Kissinger is now 75 but the chairmen of multinational corporations, such as American Express and Revlon, pay Kissinger Associates Inc., the consultancy firm he set up in 1982, millions of dollars each year to brief them on world affairs. As a statesman for hire, **he is still one of the most influential men on the planet.***

*He minimises the significance of his traumatic childhood and **his Jewish heritage -he's not a practising Jew** and describes his upbringing as middle-class German..."* End quote.

On Saturday, 4th November 1995, I received a room to room call on my hotel telephone in Jerusalem. "Turn on CNN", my friend spoke urgently. "Rabin has just been shot!" The CNN airtime was completely dedicated to the Rabin assassination. The first up to comment was Lawrence Engleberger. "We have lost a brilliant peace negotiator in the Middle East. There is only one other who could possibly follow on with the plan. I refer to Dr Kissinger."

Next to appear on the screen was none other than Kissinger himself. He was in China, setting up the re-uniting of Hong Kong with mainland China. He wept as he spoke, pointing out that he had lost a good friend in the person of Rabin. **"We will not let the peace process die"**, he said and continued on with his view of the Middle East future without Rabin.

Only those who study this man's life and sayings would pick up the number of times he used the word **"balance"** referring of course to the **"balance of power"** This term simply means that when conducting peace negotiations, the negotiator does not want either of the parties to agree to a complete peace but rather wants to balance both parties at all times on the edge of peace and war. This is called **the Hegelian Dialectic**.

The Hegelian Dialectic is a process by which Thesis combined with Antithesis ends up as Synthesis i.e.

World's leading nations	South Africa	Ireland	Middle East
Thesis - U.S.A.	ANC	Unionists	Israelis
Antithesis - Russia	Zulus	IRA	Arabs
= Synthesis - NWO	New South Africa	United Ireland	United Jerusalem

A non-religious Jew, sometimes referred to as the **"Public Relations Man for the New World Order"**. This man has for years been recognised world-wide for his skill in the field of diplomacy. Sir Henry Wooton observed that *"A diplomat is an honest man sent abroad to lie for his country."*

Kissinger points out that when conducting peace initiatives, **innuendo, subtlety and downright lies** are sometimes necessary to achieve the desired result. He also says that a full and complete 'peace' is not his aim. His key borrowed phrase is **'the balance of power'. This means that those two nations must be on the brink of peace and war at all times and are thus easier to manipulate.**

Can you believe what you are reading here? It is the lives of precious men and women created in the image of God that these rascals are playing with.

I am grateful to author William Burr, for his book "The Kissinger Transcripts - The Top Secret Talks with Beijing and Moscow". We quote in part from pages 18 and 20.

"From the moment when they first began to keep historical records, the Chinese showed a fascination with the complexities of diplomacy, with the give and take of interstate negotiation, the balancing of force and bluff, the variable power of human words to affect the onrushing course of events." **End quote.**

William Burr also spells out *"that Kissinger was a shrewd practitioner of balance of power diplomacy....Burr sees Kissinger as a vain and power hungry flatterer, or even a counter-revolutionary who tolerated human rights abuses in following along with them. The men who get killed are the ones who go against them."* **End quote.**

Henry's Third Visit to China (Transcript)

Chairman Mao: *"Do you pay attention or not to one of the subjects of Hegel's philosophy, that is the unity of opposites?"*
Secretary Kissinger: *"Very much. I was much influenced by Hegel in my philosophic thinking...Marx reversed the tendency of Hegel, but he adopted the basic theory."* **End quote.**

Becoming clearer now, isn't it?

Whilst I was conducting a series of lectures in County Armagh in Ireland during the month of October 1999, please note who came to visit Dublin at the same time.

"The Irish News", 13th October 1999 - *"Kissinger's hope for the north.*

One of the world's most famous diplomats last night spoke of his hope for lasting peace in Northern Ireland.

Dr Henry Kissinger, President Richard Nixon's secretary of state in the 1970s, also said he believed the appointment of Peter Mandelson as secretary of state was a "hopeful sign"for the peace process.

Speaking at the Independent News and Media lecture at Trinity College, Dublin, Dr Kissinger said he believed the gap between unionists and republicans could be closed.

*He said, "I think the Good Friday agreement is a hopeful step. And I think **the appointment of Mr Mandelson** is a hopeful sign because he is close to the prime minister and is highly intelligent. These are qualities that are needed to bridge what on the surface looks like a manageable gap (between unionists and republicans)."*

Dr Kissinger also said he had no ideas on how to solve the decommissioning impasse other than those put forward by senator George Mitchell, a man who he said he respected greatly." End quote.

Notice the power of this man. One moment, Mo Mowlam is in charge. Kissinger arrives and out goes Mo and in comes Peter (from the cold after being forgiven a scandal).

To Complete the Scenario

What we are looking for now is a non-religious Jewish world leader to confirm a seven year peace treaty between the Jews and the Arabs. It must happen very soon as the prophetic period known as the **Beginning of Sorrows**, starts with this peace agreement. Madeleine Albright has made it clear that the United States wants a comprehensive treaty in place by the month of September 2000.

Prophesied about 600B.C., we read these words referring to a great one world leader who is to appear about this time in history. *"And he shall confirm the covenant with many for one week (seven years) and in the midst of the week, (after three and a half years), he (the Antichrist) shall cause the sacrifice and the oblation to cease...."*[1]

Palestine Peace is Now a Nobel Cause

'The West Australian', Perth, Australia, 12th January 1999 - *"An army of Nobel Peace Prize winners and foreign political leaders gathered in Tel Aviv yesterday to demonstrate support for peace between Israelis and Palestinians...*
*The Nobel Peace laureates attending included former Soviet President Mikhail Gorbachev, South African arch-bishop Desmond Tutu, former South African president Frederik de Klerk, former Costa Rican president Oscar Sanchez and former United States secretary of state, **Henry Kissinger**, as well as former Israel prime minister Shimon Peres..."* End quote.

All is not well however, for this great world leader. He will only reign in power for three and a half years, then he meets his end. This was predicted about AD51 - *"And there was given unto him a mouth speaking great things and blasphemies, and power was given unto him to continue forty and two months (three and a half years)..."*[2] End quote.

When God's Son returns, He will wipe out this wicked being! *"And then shall that Wicked be revealed, whom the Lord shall consume with the spirit of His mouth, and shall destroy with the brightness of His coming."*[3] End quote.

---

[1]Daniel 9:27
[2]Revelation 13:5
[3]II Thessalonians 2:8

Chapter Twenty-Eight
Bringing Down the Old World Order - Where Will It All Start?

The excitement is infectious! Tens of thousands of folk from all over the world are gathering at the Millennium celebration sites. London's Millennium Dome, New York's Times Square, St Catherine's Monastery at the base of Mount Sinai, the Vatican in Rome, the Great Pyramid at Giza in Egypt, and the Chatham Islands near the international date line.

Strange Anomalies

1. The world-wide media are telling us all a deliberate lie. According to the Royal Observatory at Greenwich, on the banks of the Thames River in London, the year 2000 is the conclusion of this millennium (or 1000 year period) and **the new millennium or 1000 year period starts on the 1st January 2001.**

2. It is still unclear which country will be the first to see the sun on the 1st January 2000. 'Australian', 16th June 1999 - *"The first sunrise of 2000 will be the Australian Antarctic Territory, not New Zealand's Chatham Islands, scientists have confirmed....The problem is that the sun will have barely set the night before....Those who want to be the first to see the sun on January 1st will have to be in New Zealand's Antarctic Territory on the stroke of midnight. However, they will not see it rise because at that time of the year, the sun is always in the sky...."* End quote.

'Sunday Star Times', 28th February 1999 - *"A Russian State will enter the millennium ten minutes before the Chatham Islands, and a New Zealander will market it to the rest of the world. First Light founder, Brad Roberts, has approached the Russian government for the rights to the last millennial midnight when the state of Chukotka will enter the year 2000 two minutes before Tonga, and ten minutes before the Chatham Islands..."* End quote.

3.   'Australian', 20th August 1999 - *"Tonga has proclaimed it will have an hour of daylight saving at the end of this year in an attempt to ensure it will be the first nation to see in the new millennium, the regional Pacnews announced yesterday."* End quote.

'Herald NZ', 29th March 1999 - *"Ancient Moriori ideas about peace will be central to Millennium celebrations on the **Chatham Islands**.*

Indigenous people from around the world have been invited to a new marae (meeting ground) on the Chathams for a ceremony renewing a covenant of peace that was once unbroken for more than 500 years....

The ancestors of the Moriori observed a covenant which outlawed warfare and killing. Fighting was ritualised when first blood was drawn, honour was satisfied." End quote.

'Sunday Star Times', 31st January 1999 - *"The countdown to the mother of all New Years is on. With 11 months to go, international media is focussed on the Chatham Islands **the first inhabited place** to greet the new millennium.*

In the Chatham Islands, Mayor Patrick Smith, says accommodation is limited to just 65 commercial beds (most of which have been booked for months) and 180 houses." End quote.

'Sunday Star Times', 3rd January 1999 - *"New Zealand has been invited to strike the first match in a **beacons of fire celebration** to light up the world at midnight New Year's eve this year.*

Up to one million beacons will be lit around the globe to welcome the new millennium hour by hour as each country strikes midnight...

Midnight strikes New Zealand when it is 11.00 a.m. in London, 6.00 a.m. in New York, 8.00 p.m. in Tokyo and anywhere between 5.30 and 10.00 p.m. in Australia. No other country has this advantage...." End quote.

Okay, so all these countries are vying to be the first to see the sun and stage their parties. **Big deal!**

When the bug hits, and the lights go out, the bands which rely on electronics and amplification will strum soundless strings and an eerie quiet will precede the cries of disbelief and terror. The visitors to millennium sites will to run somewhere for help, won't they?

Another point which may influence folk to choose New Zealand over other sites. The Y2K bug will strike there at 11.00 a.m., 1st January and secondly, it will be in the midst of summer. **Pity these others who live on the opposite side of the world**.

Chapter Twenty-Nine
Prophetically Speaking - Where Are We?

1.   At a defining point when the Mystery of Iniquity is about to be fulfilled i.e. a complete change in lifestyle for the whole world as a super-world leader called Antichrist is revealed to the world. *"And now ye know what withholdeth that he might be revealed in his time. For the mystery of iniquity doth already work: only he who now letteth will let, until he be taken out of the way."*[1]

2.   **A seven year peace treaty** between the Arabs and Israel is to be brought about and confirmed by this by now recently revealed Antichrist. *"And he shall confirm the covenant with many for one week: and in the midst of the week he shall cause the sacrifice and the oblation to cease..."*[2]

        Over the years I have put off writing anything too definite on this Peace Treaty, until things became very clear. That time has come at last.

        On the 13th September 1999, the final status peace talks were held, with the date of the 13th September 2000 for the final implementation. Now, Barak, Arafat and Clinton, at their Norwegian meeting, have put the process forward to the 13th March 2000. Who knows, it may even happen sooner than that!

Please notice the continual usage of the witchcraft number - 13.

3.   The first three and a half years of this seven year period is called 'Beginning of Sorrows'. *"All these are the beginning of sorrows."*[3]

        Ten things will take place during this time (as seen in David Wilkerson's vision).

A.   A rise in false religions
B.   Wars
C.   Famines

D. Pestilence
E. Earthquakes
F. World monetary crash
G. Weather going crazy
H. Flood of filth - videos etc
I. Hate the parents crusade
J. Persecution of Christians

4. Also, about the beginning of this period of three and a half years, the millennium Y2K bug will do irreparable damage to the social, economic structure of the world system.

5. **The world's money system will collapse**.

    After this collapse, troops and police will be on duty to try and restore calm, and also to deal harshly with troublemakers. The world's food reserves at this time will be low, possibly down to about 50 days. Nations will be devastated and governments will be willing to yield up anything, even sovereignty to any person who seems to have an answer. Out of the blue, a man rises out of all this confusion, and declares, "I have the answer." He introduces a Global Bank and a new world money system.

6. The mark of the beast will be introduced i.e. a silicon chip in the right hand or forehead for buying and selling. The mark will be voluntary at this stage. *"And he causeth all, both small and great, rich and poor, free and bond, to receive a mark in their right hand, or in their foreheads: And that no man might buy or sell, save he that had the mark, or the name of the beast, or the number of his name."*[4] Predicted 96 A.D.

7. Because times will be difficult, **believers in Christ will become highly unpopular** as somehow, their supernatural God continues to provide for them, as the rest of the unbelieving world suffers. *"Let us hold fast the profession of our faith without wavering; (for He is faithful that promised;) And let us consider one another to provoke unto*

*love and to good works: Not forsaking the assembling of
ourselves together, as the manner of some is; but exhorting
one another: and so much the more, as ye see the day
approaching."*

*"But my God shall supply all your need according to
his riches in glory by Christ Jesus."*[5]

*"And thou shalt remember all the way which the Lord thy
God led thee these forty years in the wilderness, to* **humble
thee***, and to* **prove thee***, to* **know what was in thine heart***,
whether thou wouldest keep his commandments, or no. And
he humbled thee, and suffered thee to hunger, and fed thee
with manna, which thou knewest not, neither did thy fathers
know; that he might make thee know that man doth not live
by bread only, but by every word that proceedeth out of the
mouth of the Lord doth man live. Thy raiment waxed not
old upon thee, neither did thy foot swell, these forty
years."*[6]

*"Blessed is the man that walketh not in the counsel of the
ungodly, nor standeth in the way of sinners, nor sitteth in
the seat of the scornful. But his delight is in the law of
the Lord; and in His law doth he meditate day and night.
And he shall be like a tree planted by the rivers of water,
that bringeth forth his fruit in his season; his leaf also
shall not wither; and whatsoever he doeth shall prosper.
The ungodly are not so: but are like the chaff which the
wind driveth away. Therefore the ungodly shall not stand
in the judgment, nor sinners in the congregation of the
righteous. For the Lord
knoweth the way of the righteous: but the way of the
ungodly shall perish."*[7]

8.   **Earthquakes** such as those already experienced in Turkey,
        Greece, Taiwan and Mexico will become a world-wide
        feature. Only believers in Christ will have the confidence
        to stand in that day. *"Whose voice then shook the earth:
        but now He hath promised, saying, Yet once more I shake
        not the earth only, but also Heaven. And this word, Yet
        once more, signifieth the removing of those things that are*

shaken, as of things that are made, that those things which
cannot be shaken may remain."[8]

9.   **False teachers and financial extortioners will be taken
      off the preaching circuit**. *"But there were false prophets
      also among the people, even as there shall be false teachers
      among you, who privily shall bring in damnable heresies,
      even denying the Lord that bought them, and bring upon
      themselves swift destruction. And many shall follow their
      pernicious ways; by reason of whom the way of truth shall
      be evil spoken of. And through covetousness shall they
      with feigned words make merchandise of you: whose
      judgment now of a long time lingereth not, and their
      damnation slumbereth not."*[9]

10.   **The true people of God will reject the gospel of self**,
      giving to receive and will return to the preaching of
      salvation through the blood of Jesus at the cross.
      Righteousness will be a key theme. *"For if God spared not
      the angels that sinned, but cast them down to hell, and
      delivered them into chains of darkness, to be reserved unto
      judgment; And spared not the old world, but saved Noah
      the eight person, a preacher of righteousness, bringing in
      the flood upon the world of the ungodly..."*[10]
      *"For I am not ashamed of the gospel of Christ: for it is the
      power of God unto
      salvation to everyone that believeth; to the Jew first, and
      also to the Greek."*[11]
      *"For the preaching of the cross is to them that perish
      foolishness; but unto us which
      are saved it is the power of God."*[12]

11.   **We understand that Noah was saved prior to the world-
      wide flood.** *"And so it was in the days of Noe, so shall it
      be also in the days of the Son of man. They did eat, they
      drank, they married wives, they were given in marriage,
      until the day that Noe entered into the ark, and the flood
      came, and destroyed them all."*[13]

12. **Lot was delivered before the fire of judgment on Sodom and Gomorrah**. *"Likewise also as it was in the days of Lot; they did eat, they drank, they bought, they sold, they planted, they builded; But the same day that Lot went out of Sodom it rained fire and brimstone from heaven, and destroyed them all."*[14]

13. **Therefore, the born-again believers in Christ will be saved and delivered just prior to the judgment of God on an unbelieving world**. This judgment is known as the Great Tribulation. *"Even **thus** shall it be in the day when the Son of man is revealed."*[15]

14. At the conclusion of the first three and a half years called "Beginning of Sorrows", the **Lord Jesus Christ returns**, not to the earth, but **to the clouds, to take His believing, trusting, born-again beloved ones home to Heaven**. *"For the Lord Himself shall descend from Heaven with a shout, with the voice of the archangel, and with the trump of God: and the dead in Christ shall rise first: Then we which are alive and remain shall be caught up together with them in the clouds to meet the Lord in the air: and so shall we ever be with the Lord. Wherefore comfort one another with these words."*[16]

15. **He leaves the archangel Michael, on earth to protect His example nation, Israel**, during the second three and a half year period (the Great Tribulation). *"And at that time shall Michael stand up, the great prince which standeth for the children of Thy people: and there shall be a time of trouble, such as never was since there was a nation even to that same time: and at that time Thy people shall be delivered, every one that shall be found written in the book. And many of them that sleep in the dust of the earth shall awake, some to everlasting life, and some to shame and everlasting contempt."*[17]

16. A beautiful group of believers in Christ and His precious blood, made up of Jews and Gentiles, **then attend the**

marriage supper of the Lamb. Jesus is the bridegroom while the redeemed make up the bride of Christ. *"Let us be glad and rejoice, and give honour to Him: for the marriage of the Lamb is come, and His wife hath made herself ready."*[18]

17.   At this point, the world is plunged into a time of terrible trouble called Great Tribulation. Lucifer, represented by the golden cap-stone on the pyramid will control the whole world system through his two front men - the Antichrist and the False Prophet. The mark of the beast for the purposes of buying and selling becomes compulsory at this stage. Refusal to take the mark leads to the French method of execution i.e. the guillotine. *"And I saw thrones, and they sat upon them, and judgment was given unto them: and I saw the souls of them that were beheaded for the witness of Jesus, and for the word of God, and which had not worshipped the beast, neither his image, neither had received his mark upon their foreheads, or in their hands; and they lived and reigned with Christ a thousand years."*[19]

18.   The **Great Tribulation period** of the second three and a half years will be so bad that **God will shorten the days to preserve life on earth.** *"For then shall be great tribulation, such as was not since the beginning of the world to this time, no, nor ever shall be. And except those days should be shortened there should no flesh be saved: but for the elect's sake those days shall be shortened."*[20]

19.   **Meanwhile, the believers in Christ can expect a great welcome home**. Both dead and living believers will make up that vast number from every nation on earth. *"And they sung a new song, saying, Thou art worthy to take the book, and to open the seals thereof: for Thou wast slain, and hast redeemed us to God by Thy blood out of every kindred, and tongue, and people, and nation..."*[21]

20.   Having come in repentance and faith in Jesus' blood via His cross, they are **secure** in the knowledge that their

names are written in **the Family Album** entitled **"The Lamb's Book of Life".** *"And whosoever was not found written in the book of life was cast into the lake of fire."*[22]

21. **The believers in Christ and His precious blood then have their eyes opened to the eternal glories they can enjoy,** all because of the sacrifice of the Lord Jesus Christ. *"But as it is written, Eye hath not see, nor ear heard, neither have entered into the heart of man, the things which God hath prepared for them that love Him. But God hath revealed them unto us by His Spirit: for the Spirit searcheth all things, yea, the deep things of God."*[23]

22. **The unbelievers on the other hand have the horrible experience of living and suffering on earth during the Great Tribulation and then the indescribable torture of the lake of fire forever.** *"And the third angel followed them, saying with a loud voice, If any man worship the beast and his image, and receive his mark in this forehead, or in his hand, the same shall drink of the wine of the wrath of God, which is poured out without mixture into the cup of His indignation; and he shall be tormented with fire and brimstone in the presence of the holy angels, and in the presence of the Lamb: and the smoke of their torment ascendeth up forever and ever: and they have no rest day nor night, who worship the beast and his image, and whosoever receiveth the mark of his name."*[24]

Years ago, whilst at Bible School, I went for a lunch hour stroll and was glad to meet my old Bible Class teacher. After some time had passed, he posed this question. "Barry, why do people go to Hell?"

I answered, "Because they are sinners, Mr Cunningham."

"Wrong!" he replied. **"They go there because they ignore God's remedy for sin - the blood of Jesus Christ and His substitutionary death on their behalf."**

"He that believeth on the Son hath everlasting life: and he that believeth not the Son shall not see life; but the wrath of God abideth on him."[25]

---

[1]2 Thessalonians 2:6-7
[2]Daniel 9:27a
[3]Matthew 24:1-8
[4]Revelation 13:16-18
[5]Philippians 4:19
[6]Deuteronomy 8:2-4
[7]Psalm 1:1-6
[8]Hebrews 12:26-27
[9]2 Peter 2:1-3
[10]2 Peter 2:4-5
[11]Romans 1:16
[12]1 Corinthians 1:18
[13]Luke 17:26-27
[14]Luke 17:28-29
[15]Luke 17:30
[16]1 Thessalonians 4:16-18
[17]Daniel 12:1-2
[18]Revelation 19:7
[19]Revelation 20:4
[20]Matthew 24:21-22
[21]Revelation 5:9
[22]Revelation 20:15
[23]1 Corinthians 2:9-10
[24]Revelation 14:9-11
[25]John 3:36

Chapter Thirty
The Answer

I've found the answer as to why so-called intelligent people can read all this material and yet not perceive the type of problem they are facing. It is not political, economic or religious but spiritual. A luciferian, satanic, plan to take over every bodies' lives from the cradle to the grave.

To gain perceptive understanding, Jesus got it right when He said, *"Verily, verily, I say unto you, except a man be born again, He cannot see the kingdom of God."*[1]

I have had someone say to me recently, "But I don't want to be born again and mix with all those hypocrites." Unknowingly, this person just condemned themselves to miss Heaven forever (unless they change their mind). God owns Heaven. Jesus is God, not you or me! He sets the qualifications as to who will enter.

Billy Sunday, the famous preacher of the 1900's, answered that objection in this manner. "Why not mix with the hypocrites now for a short time, rather than go to Hell and be with them forever!"

When writing these books, I have presented a very strong Bible-based 'world view'. For this reason, as soon as some of my readers suspect that the Word of God is about to be mentioned, they freeze up. Their 'world view', usually heavily influenced by family, friends and teachers, doesn't allow for God at all **until many of them are on their death beds.**

It was easy for me, from the day I could begin to think for myself, to realise that, since my body was so cleverly designed, if God did not exist, I could not possibly be here. Even the most intellectually challenged among us needs to be taught a very basic axiom.

1.   Nothing creates nothing -   **correct**   **incorrect**
        (Please circle the correct answer....)

2.   Evolution goes against the 2nd law of thermodynamics, that things never improve of themselves, but always deteriorate.
3.   If God created human beings, then surely He left us a text book to show us how to operate our lives.
4.   He did! It is called the Bible, the Word of God.
5.   This book is different to any other book on the face of the earth e.g. As you travel on public transport, try reading a newspaper or an ordinary book. You will not attract any attention. **Now, open your Bible and notice the difference!**
6.   We are excited to announce that the Bible from its original pure translation can be proven to be the Word of God. It has special features that no other book has. Now, just because you wish to prove yourself a secular humanist, and intellectually superior to all this information, may I humbly suggest that at this moment, you mentally transport yourself forward in time. You are now lying on your death bed. Your breathing is slow and laboured. If you are fortunate, your family are gathered around to farewell you with their tears. You see, you are about to embark upon a journey from which there is no return. Let me assure you, having been in this very position once during my short life span, that the thing furthest from your mind at that point, will be the denial of the existence of the great Creator, Almighty God, and His gracious provision of a Saviour from our sin in the person of our Lord Jesus Christ.

"The Scriptures make it abundantly clear that the visible things we see in the world, nature that teems around us, the flowers that bloom, the sea and that within it, the birds that fly, the earth on which we live, the animals that roam its surface, and the evidence of our existence, reveal to the heart that searches, that God made all these things."[2] End quote.

*"Because that which may be known of God is manifest (apparent) in them, for God hath shewed it unto them. For the invisible things of Him from the creation of the world **are clearly seen**, being understood by the things that are made, even His eternal power and Godhead, **so that they are without excuse**."*[3] End quote.

Seven - God's Seal

The distinguished Russian mathematician, Ivan Panin, set himself the task of proving the Bible not to be the Word of God. He finally discovered that beyond a shadow of doubt, it was the Word of God. Hidden beneath the surface of the Biblical text was God's seal - the **seal of seven**. Dr Panin challenged many of the top figures of his day, to refute his findings, but nobody was willing to answer the challenge.

"God's dealings with mankind, and all life, are marked by specific design in which seven is prominent. This is even discernible in the light which comes from our sun. This pure, clear, light is made up of seven distinct colours, red, orange, yellow, green, blue, indigo and violet. Can this be an accident?

Did you know that the development of the human embryo is calculated in periods of sevens? At the 28th week, it is generally assumed a child is capable of living if born, and the date of normal birth is so calculated at 40 weeks that the physician gives this approximate date as the expected date of birth. Children born prior to this time are generally known as "pre-mature", and born beyond this time as "over-due". An accidental occurrence is it?

Birds that have been checked out as being involved in this remarkable seal of seven also stand out.

....It is well-known that when eggs are set under a domestic hen, or even if they are placed in an incubator, one looks for chicks on the 21st day. Check up on your canary at 14 days. Hundreds of finches of all varieties and numerous other families of small birds like robins, thrushes and cockatoos have been checked out at 14 days also, and there are many other bird families with incubation periods in multiples of seven.

...These periods are by definite appointment, namely that in a given family, the periods extend exactly by seven.

God's dealings with man are in sevens, and if you study dispensations in the Bible, you will find there are seven distinct periods of God's dealings with man on the earth. We are now in the closing days of the sixth, called ***"grace"***.

No.7 in the Bible is most important. In the book of Revelation we read of seven churches, seven Spirits of God, seven candlesticks, seven stars, seven seals, seven angels, seven trumpets, seven thunders, 42 months=6x7. Three and a half years with two witnesses, 7000 men killed by an earthquake, seven heads, seven crowns, Beast with seven heads, seven plagues, seven mountains, seven kings.

The Seal Beneath the Surface

*Panin's work has been investigated by the **Nobel Research Foundation of Los Angeles, U.S.A.** and regarding his statement that **the Bible could not possibly have been written except by inspiration of God Himself** and their verdict is as follows: **"So far as our investigation has proceeded, we find the evidence overwhelmingly in favour of such a statement".** "*[4] End quote.

N.B. **Every letter in the Hebrew alphabet has a corresponding numeric value.**

For the purpose of encouraging our readers to investigate these claims further, we include one last example of God's Seal on His Word. *"The vital opening words of **Genesis1:1. "In the beginning God created the heavens and the earth."** These words are the very foundation of God's Word. If He were going to seal any words, surely He would seal these, and seal them He has!*

•*The verse consists of exactly seven Hebrew words*	*7*
•*These seven words have exactly 28 letters*	*4 x 7*
•*There are three nouns - God, heaven, earth. Total numeric value - 777*	*3 x 7*
•*There is one Hebrew verb - "created". Its numeric value is 203*	*29 x 7*
•*The first three Hebrew words contain the subject - 14 letters*	*2 x 7*
•*The fourth and fifth words have exactly 7 letters*	*7*
•*The sixth and seventh words have exactly 7 letters*	*7*
•*The Hebrew words for the two objects, the heaven, the earth, 7 letters each*	*7*
•*The value of the first, middle and last letters in the verb "created" - 133*	*19 x 7*
•*The numeric value of the first and last letters of the 7 words is 1393*	*199 x 7*
•*The value of the first and last letters of the verse is 497*	*71 x 7*
•*So the value of the first and last letters of the words between is 896*	*128 x 7*
•*The Hebrew particle "ETH" with article THE is used twice - 406*	*58 x 7*
•*The last letters of the first and last words = 490*	*70 x 7*

*It has been found that there are over thirty different numeric features in the verses and calculated that **the chance of coincidence for the above is 15:1 in thirty three trillion odd.***

Some of the world's foremost mathematicians, after studying it, have concluded that not even the cleverest man who ever lived could have devised such a sublime mathematical problem and hide it in such a simple statement that declares the first stupendous miracle of God.

Hidden within itself is not only found the seal of seven, but also a mathematical key to unlock every aspect of its fundamental truths, some of which were not known to man until the advent of Christ.

Hebrews 1:2 - "....spoken unto us by His Son....by Whom also He made the worlds"." End quote.

I hope all this whets your appetite for more of the same. This author personally enjoys all this information as **God's seal is only found in the original Scriptures from Genesis to Malachi in the Hebrew language and from Matthew to Revelation in the Greek language.**

The seal cannot be found in the Apocrypha, the Koran, the Book of Mormon or any other book - just the Bible. **Let no-one become angry**. It is important when dealing with facts of a spiritual nature to humble one's self and learn.

What We Have Learned

Only the spiritual man or woman can possibly understand the New World Order luciferian conspiracy and the satanic nature of Freemasonry. Any man, be he a layman or a clergyman, can rant, rave and shout, yet this simply proves that **he is still a natural man, in desperate need of a touch from the Lord**.

"But the natural man receiveth the things of the Spirit of God, for they are foolishness unto him, neither can he know them because they are spiritually discerned. But he that is spiritual judgeth all things...."[5]

For any reader who struggles with the King James 1611 English above, let us look at the Amplified Version taken from the original Greek language with many added facets of meaning.

"But the natural, non-spiritual man does not accept or welcome or admit into his heart the gifts and teachings and revelations of the Spirit of God, for they are folly (meaningless nonsense) to him, and he is incapable of knowing them (of progressively recognising, understanding, and becoming better acquainted with them) because they are spiritually discerned. But the spiritual man tries all things (he examines, investigates, enquires into, questions and discerns all things)." End quote.

Excuse the question but which one are you?

Natural man or woman - never been born-again of God's`Spirit.
Spiritual man or woman - thoroughly born-again of God's Spirit.
A **religious** man or woman or a **relationship** man or woman?

The difference is amazingly clear once your life is touched by the finger of God. In New Zealand each Sunday morning, there is a half hour programme of hymn-singing using a wide cross section of choirs and groups from all over the country. A 'twice-born' believer in the Lord Jesus Christ can see the two groups so easily portrayed. When the 'born-agains' sing, our hearts light up and sing in unison with them.

A Final Story

A gypsy boy and his mother travelling by horse and cart came to a wide, rushing river in the midst of a fearsome storm. The horse, not realising the bridge had been washed away plunged into the raging torrent. The old lady was flung upstream and as she got caught in the strong current, she tried to swim to save herself. Her shawl, filled with water, made this impossible.

The boy cried, "Mother, grab my hand" and reached out to save her. She ignored him and carried on swimming. She was swept away into the darkness.

They locked the boy in a padded cell and passers by would hear him crying day and night, **"Mother, I tried to save you but you wouldn't let me."**

Jesus has given His life's blood to save you. **Will you let Him?**

"For God so loved the world * (your name)..................................., that He gave His only begotten Son (Jesus), that whosoever * (your name)................................ believeth in Him (Jesus) should not perish (or go to Hell), but have (not wait for, hope or think about) everlasting life."[6]

It is as clear as that.

The Bible teaches that there are three steps, plus one, to possess this life from God. Find a quiet place and kneel down or get into an attitude of prayer (sit if necessary).

Start praying - here are the three steps:

1. Repent of your sin. Turn to Jesus.
2. Believe that He died for you.
3. Receive Him - invited Him into your heart - plus -
4. Tell someone what you have done.

If you find that you do not know how to pray, here is the prayer of Salvation.

Part One

(Say out loud) "Lord Jesus Christ, I come to you now, because I am a sinner. Today, Lord Jesus, I repent of my sin, I turn away from my sin, and I turn to you."

Part Two

"I believe, dear Lord, that You died for me * (your name)........................and I thank you Lord, because your blood covers all my sins. No one else can save me, only Jesus."

Part Three

"Right now, I open the door of my heart (put your hand to your chest and open outwards). Come into my heart, Lord Jesus. Wash me. Cleanse me, and make me Your child. I receive you now by faith.

Help me to live for you every day until you come again.

I close the door (use your hand again, bring it back towards your chest) and Jesus is inside.

I thank you, Lord Jesus, because today, by faith, I have received You and You have received me.

Amen."

Here is the promise:

"To as many (anybody) as received Him (Jesus), to them gave He power to become the Sons of God." John 1:12.

Your choice this day gives you that power, and right, to call yourself a Son of God - praise Him now in your own words.

Please fill in the certificate on the back page and then;

1.   Copy it out again on to the front page of your Bible
2.   Send another copy to me immediately so I can send you further assistance.
3.   Go and tell someone what you have done.

"That if thou shalt confess with thy MOUTH, the Lord Jesus, and shalt believe in thine HEART that God has raised Him from the dead, thou shalt be saved." Romans 10:9. (Emphasis added.)

That which is in your heart, must come out your mouth. This is your starting point.

Now; steps to help you continue on for Christ -

1.   Pray daily
2.   Read your Bible daily. Start in John's gospel because it speaks about salvation and everlasting life.
3.   Witness, or tell others about Christ.
4.   Link up with a Bible-based church or Christian group.

Welcome to the Family of God. I look forward to meeting you up there.

Your friend

Barry Smith

New Birth Certificate

At (time)......................... on (date)..

I (name)...

received the Lord Jesus Christ as my own Saviour. I thank Him.

Signed...

---

[1]John 3:3
[2]"The Seal of God" by F.G. Payne - page 3
[3]Romans 1:19-20
[4]"The Seal of God" by F.G. Payne
[5]1 Corinthians 2:14-15
[6]John 3:16